CAPE WINELANDS Cuisine

First edition 2011
By Human & Rousseau
An imprint of NB Publishers
40 Heerengracht, Cape Town, 8000

Human & Rousseau
Cape Town Pretoria

Commissioning Editor:
Daleen van der Merwe

Editor and indexer:
Joy Clack/Bushbaby Editorial Services

Translator: Laetitia Sullivan/Bushbaby
Editorial Services

Design: Infestation

Photography: Mickey Hoyle

Styling: Jacques Erasmus

Food preparation:
Chris Erasmus, Michelle Theron

Proofreader: Samantha Fick/Bushbaby
Editorial Services

Reproduction by Infestation

Printed and bound by Tien Wah Press (Pte) Ltd,
Singapore

ISBN 978-0-7981-5222-8

CAPE WINELANDS
Cuisine

COMPILED BY HETTA VAN DEVENTER-TERBLANCHE

Human & Rousseau
Cape Town Pretoria

CONTENTS

CAPE WINELANDS MAP

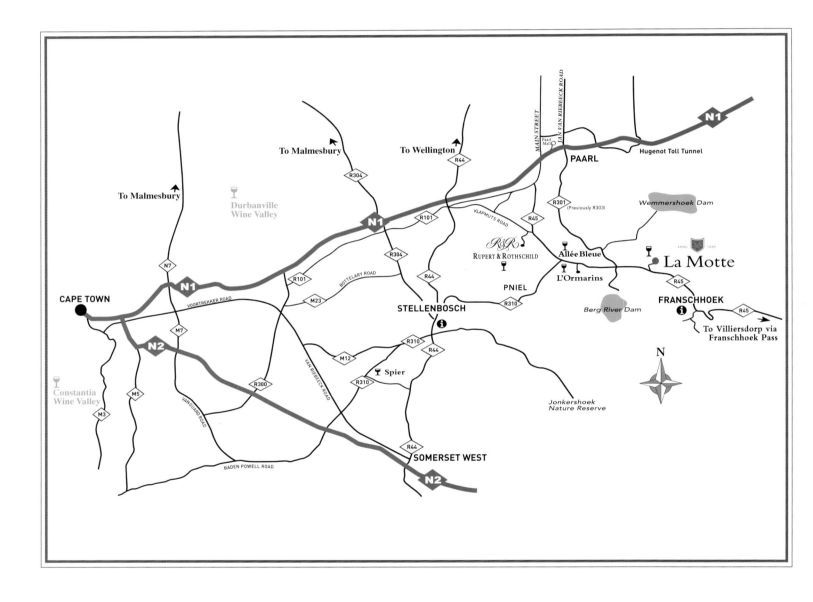

map

6

FOREWORD

Dear Reader,

The book that you hold in your hands is the loving result of the efforts of many dedicated people who share a common passion for the cuisine of South Africa's Cape Winelands.

The Winelands, with their magnificent landscapes of craggy mountains and sprawling vineyards, holds the combined history of many different nationalities who, over the centuries, travelled to this southernmost part of Africa to start a new life. Here they adapted the recipes of their distant homelands to their new surroundings and shared their culinary skills with one another. *Cape Winelands Cuisine* is the result of this culinary collaboration which passed from one generation to the next in the form of recipes unique to the region. It is our interpretation of these wonderful recipes that we share with you in this book.

Honouring our heritage through modern interpretation is very much the philosophy of La Motte, our wine estate in the Franschhoek Valley region of the Cape Winelands, where the idea for this book was conceived. Rediscovering Cape Winelands cuisine was a natural extension of the journey we have undertaken with our wines, notably the Shiraz and Sauvignon Blanc varietals. At La Motte, our love of the land is not only confined to wine and food, but extends to indigenous flowers and ethereal oils.

There are many people to thank for this book, and to all of you we extend our heartfelt appreciation for your efforts and passion. There are a few people who deserve special mention.

Foremost is Hetta van Deventer, La Motte's culinary manager and author of this book. Hetta has been the driving force behind this book, applying years of research to experimentation and innovation with the culinary team at Pierneef à La Motte, our estate restaurant which serves many of the recipes contained in this book. Working alongside Hetta on the development of the recipes has been head Chef de Cuisine Chris Erasmus and Sous Chef Michelle Theron.

The historic foundation for the book was provided by Dr Hester W. Claassens (author of *Die Geskiedenis van Boerekos 1652–1806*), who undertook the first scientific research into the origins of the cuisine of South Africa's settlers from Europe. Dr Claassens was also tireless in checking the historical facts of the book, providing a sounding board for ideas, and helping to adapt the historic recipes for this book.

Thanks are also due to the wonderful team who helped bring this book to life. Commissioning editor Daleen van der Merwe from Human & Rousseau, photographer Mickey Hoyle, stylist Jacques Erasmus, translator Laetitia Sullivan, editor Joy Clack and proofreader Samantha Fick.

The final thanks is to you, the reader, for wanting to share this magical celebration of Cape Winelands cooking with us. We hope that you derive as much pleasure from reading and using the book as we did in compiling it.

Hein Hanneli

Hein & Hanneli Koegelenberg

INTRODUCTION

The Cape Winelands, also known as the Boland, includes the traditional wine-producing districts of Constantia, Stellenbosch, Franschhoek, Paarl, Wellington, Worcester and Tulbagh. The recipes in this book are based on recipes that developed over more than three centuries in these same areas, with emphasis on the very first and oldest recipes that were brought to the Cape by European settlers in the seventeenth century.

The origins of Cape Winelands cuisine can be traced back to when Jan van Riebeeck established a refreshment station at the Cape in 1652, by order of the Dutch East India Company. The station was to provide ships with fresh produce for the long sea voyage around the tip of Africa. The Europeans at the Cape, comprising mainly German-speaking, Dutch, Flemish and French people, among others, established a culture of cooking with wine and a vast variety of European as well as Middle and Far Eastern herbs and spices, in the same way as their European contemporaries. Coriander, aniseed, fennel, bay leaves, cumin, caraway, mustard and saffron featured in the kitchens and medicine supplies of European cooks for centuries before they had access to Eastern spices, such as pepper, cinnamon, nutmeg, mace, ginger, cardamom and cloves.

During the time of Jan van Riebeeck's arrival at the Cape, the French began to take the lead in Europe with regard to *haute cuisine* and innovative cooking by doing away with excessive spices and concentrating instead on highlighting the natural taste of food. Many of the French Huguenots who came to the Cape settled on farms such as La Motte in Olifantshoek (later renamed Franschhoek). They added a wealth of recipes to Cape cuisine, including recipes for stews (*bredies*), meringues and macaroons, puff and flaky pastry, the use of a bouquet garni, and Hollandaise sauce.

Although new developments in cooking were taking place in Europe, not all these methods and ideas reached the Cape and, as such, many of the old customs from Europe were preserved. Despite this, cooks at the Cape had to improvise and adapt recipes according to the available ingredients, and this presented opportunities for some very creative local cooking. Adaptations included reducing excessiveness in recipes, but while their European counterparts were cutting back on the spices, Cape cooks continued to use them in their cooking.

With the establishment of the refreshment station, Jan van Riebeeck and his fellow settlers didn't just establish a new type of culinary art at the Cape, but also added a wealth of new plants from remote corners of the world to be used in Cape cuisine. The Company's Garden was the source of an almost overwhelming assortment of fruit trees, vegetables, nuts, herbs and spices. Because there was initially a shortage of meat, the cooks at the Cape focused on preparing vegetable dishes, paving the way for a unique style of cooking at the Cape. Some of the edible wild plants of the indigenous people were also cultivated or collected in the veld and prepared according to European recipes.

In this book, the focus is largely on the old Cape's use of herbs, spices and cooking with wine, using tried-and-trusted techniques and bringing the love for sweet-and-sour dishes and the preference of serving sweet with savoury dishes back to the table. Attention is drawn to old, forgotten recipes such as homemade ravioli and pasta, of which only *melksnysels* (milk noodles) survived the journey into today's food culture.

The cooks at the Cape also didn't use synthetic seasoning and flavouring agents, as the recipes in this book show. An aromatic sauce recipe with ingredients such as crushed crayfish shells, anchovies, shallots, wine and spices was discovered among the brittle pages of a handwritten cookbook dating from 1770. Spoonfuls of the sauce can be added to soups or other dishes to enhance the flavour and, according to the author, it could be kept for up to three years. Dried and powdered mushrooms were also used as seasoning in dishes or sprinkled over for extra flavour. Various original recipes for curry mixes were found in old cookbooks and manuscripts, as recorded in one of the old manuscripts: 'om kerrie kruiden te maken'. These curry mixes were used to prepare the aromatic, mild curries favoured in the home countries of Van Riebeeck and his fellow settlers.

Through the centuries, all the many cultures making up the colourful nation of South Africa contributed in one way or another to the further development of this region's cookery. *Cape Winelands Cuisine* embodies these 'lost' recipes and 'forgotten' knowledge contained in collected favourite and family recipes, as well as the trends, cultures, flavours and events from which the pleasure of enjoying food developed here at the most southern tip of Africa.

Come and enjoy this journey through the Cape Winelands with us. Bon appétit!

BREAD

The first wheat bread served at the Cape was the hard, dried-out bread that formed part of the rations given to Dutch merchant sailors. During the long sea voyages, even this hard bread became mouldy and, for this reason, the sailors were later provided with *beskuit* (rusks).

The word *beskuit* comes from the French *biscuit de guerre*, which the French soldiers received as part of their rations. The people at the Cape referred to these rusks as *beschuit* rather than using the Dutch word *tweebak*, meaning 'baked twice'. These rusks consisted of a mixture of flour and water, but according to the author Kolbe, they were so hard that it was impossible to bite off a piece. It must have been torture for hungry scurvy sufferers with their sore gums and loose teeth to try and eat these rusks!

Through the centuries, bread has been a basic staple food for people of all cultures. Before leavening agents became widely available, this staple food consisted of a type of unleavened bread where air was the only leavening agent used when kneading. Later, beer breweries provided the yeast for baking bread. The bread at the Cape was made with hop yeast, but Van Riebeeck had to rely on imported hops. People who lived far from a brewery would use anything that could ferment, such as corn, peas, beans and barley. The French, who were famous for their superior quality bread, used salt-rising yeast and must for their bread and cakes.

The Cape was probably the first place where proper rusks were baked. Usually, one or two pans of dough for baking rusks together with a batch of dough for baking bread was placed in a large outdoor oven. The dough for the rusks consisted of bread dough mixed with extra fat. When these rusks – known as *boerbeskuit* – were removed from the oven, they were quickly broken up into smaller pieces and put back in the oven to dry out. Ingredients such as crackling, raisins, aniseed, coriander, cumin or caraway seeds were often kneaded into the *boerbeskuit* dough together with fat to give the rusks a more aromatic flavour. Eggs and sugar were sometimes used to bake *boerbeskuit*, but over time these types of rusks acquired other names.

Boerbeskuit became very popular among sailors visiting the Cape. The authority governing the Cape during that time put up a notice on 4 March 1760, banning traders at the Cape from selling any baked products to the French navy, but approximately 30 000 pounds of rusks had already been sold!

Grandmother's bread

This modern version of the recipe uses instant dry yeast instead of the salt-rising yeast used in the original. Mrs Huberte Rupert found this easy bread recipe ca. 1960 on a packet of flour she bought from Haldenwang Bakery in Bird Street, Stellenbosch, and it soon became a family favourite. She passed the recipe on to a certain Johanna, the cook at Lanzerac, from where its popularity spread across the country.

MAKES: 1 large loaf or 6 individual loaves

ingredients

1 Tbsp (15 ml) honey

2–3 tsp (10–15 ml) vegetable oil

3 cups (750 ml) lukewarm water

5 cups (5 x 250 ml) wholewheat flour (nutty wheat)

2 tsp (10 ml) salt

1 pkt (10 g) instant dry yeast

sunflower seeds and/or linseed and/or dill (optional)

extra vegetable oil, for brushing

method

Add the honey and vegetable oil to the water and stir until the honey dissolves.

In a large mixing bowl, combine the flour, salt, yeast and seeds (keep some seeds to sprinkle on top). Stir the honeyed water into the flour mixture until it is lump free and forms a stiff dough, similar to the consistency of a fruitcake batter.

Leave the mixture to rest in the mixing bowl for about 1 hour before stirring again, and then turn out the dough into a large greased bread pan or 6 smaller pans.

Preheat the oven to 200 °C (400 °F).

When the dough has risen to double the size, sprinkle with water and then the extra seeds, if using, and bake for 45 minutes. Reduce the oven temperature to 180 °C (350 °F) and bake for another 30 minutes. (For the smaller loaves, bake at 180 °C [350 °F] for 45 minutes.)

As soon as the bread is removed from the oven, brush with oil, and then place on a wire rack to cool.

Pot bread

This recipe gets it name from the traditional way of preparing the bread in a cast-iron pot placed over the coals. We have adapted it to make it easier to prepare in your oven at home.

MAKES: 2 medium loaves

ingredients

6 cups (6 x 250 ml) cake flour

¼ cup (60 ml) sugar

1 Tbsp (15 ml) salt

2 pkts (10 g each) instant dry yeast

1 Tbsp (15 ml) lamb's fat or butter

1¼ cups (300 ml) lukewarm milk

⅓ cup (80 ml) sweet potato purée

2 eggs

2 tsp (10 ml) extra lamb's fat or butter

method

Sift the flour, sugar and salt together and sprinkle the yeast over.

In a separate bowl, melt the 1 Tbsp (15 ml) lamb's fat or butter in the lukewarm milk. Add the sweet potato purée and eggs and beat well.

Add the milk mixture to the dry ingredients and mix until a soft dough is formed. Knead until smooth and elastic.

Set aside in a warm place until double in size, then knead again lightly.

Preheat the oven to 180 °C (350 °F) and grease 2 round loaf pans with butter or lamb's fat. Divide the dough equally between the loaf pans and set aside to rise until doubled in size.

Bake for 30–40 minutes until golden brown, then remove from the oven and turn out onto a wire rack to cool slightly. Smear the extra lamb's fat or butter over the top of the loaves while they are still warm.

This recipe can also be prepared in a cast-iron pot placed on the coals, with a few coals scattered on the lid.

Mosbeskuit

Mosbeskuit is a traditional rusk made with must or raisin yeast.

MAKES: 120 rusks (5 large loaves)

YEAST
ingredients

4 cups (4 x 250 ml) cake flour

6 cups (1.5 litres) fermenting must

method

Sift the cake flour into the liquid and stir until it is free of lumps and forms a smooth paste.

OR
IF MUST IS UNAVAILABLE, MAKE RAISIN YEAST

ingredients

6 cups (1.5 litres) boiling water

500 g raisins (with seeds),
pounded in a mortar with a pestle

1 tsp (5 ml) instant yeast

1 Tbsp (15 ml) sugar

4 cups (4 x 250 ml) cake flour

method

Pour the boiling water over the pounded raisins and set aside until lukewarm. Add the yeast and sugar. Stir to dissolve, pour into a glass jar and cover. Let it rest overnight in a warm place.

After 1–2 days (depending on the room temperature), when all the raisins have floated to the surface, strain the mixture through a sieve.

Sift the cake flour into the strained liquid and stir until it is free of lumps and forms a smooth paste.

DOUGH
ingredients

5 kg cake flour, sifted (± 41 cups)

1 Tbsp (15 ml) salt

1.5 kg (7½ cups) sugar

2 Tbsp (30 ml) aniseed

yeast or raisin yeast

extra flour to sprinkle on top

500 g butter or lard, melted

3 cups (750 ml) lukewarm milk or water

2 eggs

method

Sift the 5 kg cake flour, salt, sugar and aniseed together. Make a well in the centre and carefully pour in the yeast or raisin yeast; do not stir. Sprinkle the top with a little flour and leave to rise for 1 hour in a warm place.

Mix together the melted butter or lard and the milk. Whisk in the eggs. Add this to the flour mixture and knead well to a firm dough.

Form the dough into buns and pack closely together in greased bread pans. Let it rise until doubled in height, brush a little milk over the top and then bake for about 1 hour in a preheated oven at 200 °C (400 °F).

When done, leave to cool slightly in the pans before turning out. Break apart, arrange the pieces on baking trays and dry in a slow oven at 70–80 °C (160–180 °F) overnight. Or serve fresh (as *mosbolletjies*) with butter and *moskonfyt*.

BREAKFAST

Traditionally, breakfast at the Cape consisted of meat and/or fish and eggs. *Boerewors* (a type of sausage), which has become a national favourite, *boulogne* sausage (polony), pork sausage, chicken sausage, liver sausage, blood pudding, pannas and *rolpens* (*andoelie*) were popular at the breakfast table. Everyday food supplies in the home included *kaiings* (crisply fried sheep's tail fat), often used in soup and rusks, but it also formed part of the first meal of the day when served warm on bread and porridge.

Poultry was initially scarce at the Cape and therefore the eggs of various wild and sea birds, especially seagulls and penguins, were used instead. Penguin eggs were commercially available until as recently as the mid-1960s. These eggs have a slight greenish tinge, with a light salty flavour. Another striking feature of penguin eggs is that the egg white remains transparent, even when cooked and set. Today, the only eggs still used in food preparation are chicken, duck, goose and ostrich eggs.

In the past, fried, boiled, scrambled and curried eggs were served for breakfast, along with fried and smoked pork or hippopotamus bacon or meat. Eggs were even baked and served inside small green pumpkins (maranka), melons and oranges. Cumin is indigenous to the eastern areas surrounding the Mediterranean and consequently the Dutch were very familiar with its uses. Recipes for eggs served with cumin sauce appear in old Dutch cookbooks. Omelettes with various fillings, such as oysters, ham and bacon were also popular. A true South African omelette was made from ostrich egg with a biltong (dried meat) filling. An ostrich egg is equivalent to 22–24 chicken eggs and was therefore popular with large households.

The entrails of animals – the liver, kidneys, spleen, *sweserik* (sweetbread), heart (if it was a young animal) and intestines or caul stuffed with liver – were often grilled over the coals. Other delicacies on the breakfast menu were the pluck – lungs included – served minced with a sour pepper sauce, *sult* (brawn), and pan-fried liver and kidneys prepared with a sweet-and-sour sauce. Small cakes made of liver, meat, fish, oysters, crayfish and potatoes were very popular for breakfast and *frikkadelle* (meatballs), oysters, fish or pieces of cooked offal dipped in batter and fried in fat also made a regular appearance at breakfast time. Marrow on toast was always a favourite.

A traditional Cape breakfast wouldn't have been complete without serving fish, such as harder (mullet), hottentot (bronze bream) or snoek, which was usually fried in fat, braised or grilled over the coals. During the seventeenth century it was customary in the Netherlands to serve sweet turnips with fish. At the Cape, small sweet potatoes baked in warm ash replaced the turnips served with fish at breakfast.

Porridge was regularly served as a breakfast dish. Until the twentieth century, *gortpap* (barley porridge) with raisins, rice porridge prepared with milk, and a porridge made from coarsely ground flour were popular. To what extent *mieliepap* (maize porridge) was made remains uncertain because recipes for porridge were not written down. Another porridge served in the morning was made by cooking and thickening the flesh of *makataan* (wild watermelon) with flour.

Bacon tart

Many versions of bacon tart appear in old cookbooks. All the recipes are basically a variation on a salty 'bread pudding' made from egg custard, bread and breakfast bacon or ham. This recipe is a firm favourite and can easily be prepared in a large pie dish for a group of people, or as individual portions.

SERVES: 6

ingredients

3 Tbsp (45 ml) butter or lamb's tail fat

¼ cup (60 ml) dried breadcrumbs

butter or oil for sautéing

½ red onion, finely chopped

1 clove garlic, chopped

300 g back or shoulder bacon, diced

6 slices bread

4 eggs

2 cups (500 ml) buttermilk or full-cream milk (buttermilk has a distinctive sour taste)

½ cup (125 ml) grated Cheddar cheese

¼ tsp (1 ml) ground allspice

pinch of cayenne pepper

salt and freshly ground black pepper

2 spring onions, chopped, for garnishing (optional)

method

Preheat the oven to 160 °C (325 °F).

Grease an ovenproof dish with 1 Tbsp (15 ml) of the butter or lamb's tail fat and dust with the breadcrumbs. Refrigerate for 15 minutes to set.

Heat a little butter or oil in a pan and sauté the onion, garlic and bacon for 5 minutes until done.

Spread each slice of bread, on one side only, with the remaining butter or fat. Place the buttered bread in layers in the dish, buttered side up, sprinkling the sautéed onion and bacon mixture over each layer.

Mix the eggs, buttermilk or milk, cheese, allspice and cayenne pepper together. Season to taste with salt and black pepper. Pour the mixture over the bread in the ovenproof dish and bake for 15–20 minutes until golden and set. Sprinkle with spring onions (if using).

Either turn out and serve in slices, or serve directly from the dish.

Wentelteefjes

(French toast) with flavoured dried fruit compôte

This dish can be traced back more than 2 000 years to a Roman chef called Apicius, who cooked for the aristocracy during the time of Christ. Where and when the name French toast was created is uncertain; however, it was definitely part of Cape cuisine from the very beginning. The Dutch word for French toast is *wentelteefjes*. A recipe for French toast under the name *wenteljefies* can still be found in Hildagonda Duckitt's Cape cookbook.

Dried fruit compôte was a breakfast dish or an accompaniment to meat, and was also served as dessert with custard.

SERVES: 4

FRENCH TOAST
ingredients

3 eggs

½ cup (125 ml) milk

¼ tsp (1 ml) ground cinnamon

pinch of ground cloves

¼ tsp (1 ml) salt

rosemary or *kapokbos* (wild rosemary),
finely chopped

4 slices day-old bread

2 Tbsp (30 ml) butter or oil

3 rashers crisp-fried belly bacon per person
(optional)

method

Beat the eggs, milk, spices, salt and herbs together.

Soak the bread in the egg mixture for 1 minute.

Heat a mineral (stainless steel) pan, melt the butter or oil and add the soaked bread. Fry on both sides over moderate heat until golden brown and the egg in the centre of the bread is cooked through. (Sprinkle with cinnamon sugar if it is to be eaten on its own.)

DRIED FRUIT COMPÔTE
ingredients

1 cup (250 ml) sugar or honey, or according to taste

4 cups (1 litre) boiling water

2 orange leaves (optional)

juice and zest of 2 oranges

juice and zest of 1 lemon

2 rooibos teabags

3 star anise

1 cinnamon stick

2 whole cloves

3 cardamom pods

400 g mixed dried fruit

method

Dissolve the sugar or honey in the boiling water in a saucepan. Add the orange leaves, if using, the orange and lemon juices and zests, rooibos teabags and the spices. Boil for 5 minutes until syrupy.

Pour the boiling syrup over the fruit and leave overnight to infuse.

Reheat the soaked and infused fruit compôte and serve with the warm French toast and bacon.

The stewed fruit can be refrigerated in an airtight container for up to two weeks and is an excellent breakfast dish, accompanied with yoghurt and muesli.

Pannas

with sweet-and-sour pomegranate sauce

Pannas was an old German breakfast dish made from the pluck, brains and pork blood. Because of the growing aversion to the use of blood in food, *pannas* gradually developed into a dish made from liver.

The well-known South African culinary icon C. Louis Leipoldt gives a nostalgic description of this breakfast dish in his book, *Leipoldt's Food and Wine*. He writes that *pannas* was already losing its popularity during his lifetime. Today, though, it seems as if it is still being prepared in some parts of the Karoo and a cookbook recently compiled by Elsa van Schalkwyk from the Karoo contains a recipe for it. It is interesting to note that in her recipe for *pannas* she uses no blood and sheep's trotters and offal instead of liver as indicated in traditional Cape recipes. Written and copied by hand, this book contains a collection of Karoo recipes of the congregation of the Williston Dutch Reformed Church.

SERVES: 6

ingredients

¼ cup (60 ml) butter

2 cups (500 ml) diced lamb's liver

½ cup (125 ml) diced lamb's heart and kidneys (optional)

1 cup (250 ml) diced back or shoulder bacon

1 pig's trotter

1 bay leaf

1 tsp (5 ml) finely chopped fresh ginger

1 onion, finely chopped

1 clove garlic

½ tsp (2.5 ml) chopped rosemary

½ tsp (2.5 ml) freshly ground black pepper

¼ tsp (1 ml) grated nutmeg

¼ tsp (1 ml) ground cloves

zest of 1 lemon (optional)

salt

2 Tbsp (30 ml) chopped parsley

± 1 cup (250 ml) cake flour

method

Heat a medium saucepan and brown the butter lightly. Add the liver, heart, kidneys and bacon and sauté until done. Mince or chop finely.

In a heavy-based saucepan, place the pig's trotter, bay leaf, ginger, onion, garlic, rosemary, pepper, nutmeg, cloves and lemon zest. Season with salt. Add enough water to cover and bring to the boil. Reduce the heat and simmer for 1½ hours. Strain the trotter water through a sieve, retaining the water.

Add enough trotter water to the cooked and minced liver mixture until it forms a thin, porridge-like consistency. Add the chopped parsley and season to taste with salt and pepper.

Transfer the mixture to the saucepan and bring to the boil. Reduce the heat and let it simmer for 10 minutes, stirring all the while.

Add the cake flour, stirring continuously until the consistency is that of a thick porridge. Keep stirring or it will burn and form lumps.

Pour the mixture into a prepared and greased terrine mould or loaf pan (2.5 litres). Leave in a cool place for a few hours to set. A layer of fat will form on top, which will preserve the pannas.

To serve, fry thick slices in butter or lard, crumbed or without crumbs, with sage and garlic for flavour, and serve with sweet-and-sour pomegranate sauce (see page 135) or prepared mustard.

Kalkoenkos

In times gone by, a woman's worth in the kitchen was highly valued. A prized virtue was being able to prepare a fruit salad by chopping fruit into small cubes of equal size, as for a sambal. This was known as *engelenkos* (angel food). When the fruit was chopped into bigger cubes by a lazy housewife, it was called *kalkoenkos* (turkey food)!

SERVES: ¾ cup (190 ml) chopped fruit per person

ingredients

Use any available and seasonal fresh fruit, such as prickly pear, granadilla (passion fruit), guava, prunes, peaches, apples, pears, melon, pawpaw (papaya), banana, apricots, grapes or berries

method

Peel, de-pip and chop the fruit.

Squeeze over the juice of 1 orange.

Sprinkle with chopped fresh mint (optional).

Serve with granola, yoghurt, cream cheese or lavender cream (see Note below).

NOTE:

If you have to prepare the fruit in advance, do the following to prevent discoloration:

Squeeze lemon juice over apple cubes. Sprinkle with a little sugar to compensate for the extra acidity.

Pour boiling water over unpeeled bananas and set aside until the skins become black. Peel and slice.

To make 1 cup (250 ml) lavender cream – enough for 10 servings – whip 1 cup (250 ml) fresh cream with 3 Tbsp (45 ml) sugar (or to taste), and fold in ½ tsp (2.5 ml) chopped fresh lavender flowers or a pinch of chopped dried lavender flowers.

Boerewors

Every seventeenth-century cook at the Cape had a favourite recipe for *boerewors* (farmer's sausage). During the twentieth century, many cooks began following recipes that predominantly used coriander and cloves as seasoning. A possible reason for this preference might have been the Afrikaans cookbooks by Dijkman and D.J.H., which contain recipes with these spices as ingredients.

It is a popular myth that *boerewors* was always made from a mixture of pork and other meats. Before the twentieth century when there were no fridges, *boerewors* prepared in summer consisted mainly of mutton and sheep's tail fat and in winter it was made from pork and bacon.

It boggles the mind that people made sausage at all without the luxury of mincing machines. The sausage meat had to be cut into very small pieces and mixed with the spices the night before. The following morning, when it was still cold, the fat or bacon was cut into cubes while the meat was finely minced with a large pestle. Then the meat and fat or bacon were mixed with vinegar and left for a while in order to absorb the spices before cleaned intestines were filled with the meat.

It was a huge job to scrape the intestines clean. If the one doing the scraping was clumsy, the intestines ended up with lots of holes, making them useless as sausage casings. Filling the intestines also had to be done by hand. The cheapest piece of filling equipment over which the intestines could be pulled and filled with meat stuffing was the horn of an animal. The sharp end of the horn was cut off and the horn hollowed out, rubbed and polished until smooth before it was used as a filling mechanism. After the intestines were filled, the *boerewors* had to be placed in brine to preserve it.

SERVES: 8–10

ingredients

1.5 kg beef, minced

1.5 kg pork, minced

500 g pork back fat, coarsely minced or cut into small cubes

10 tsp (50 ml) whole coriander seeds

1 Tbsp (15 ml) salt

1 tsp (5 ml) freshly ground black pepper

½ tsp (2.5 ml) ground cloves

½ tsp (2.5 ml) grated nutmeg

3 Tbsp (45 ml) ground allspice

½ cup (125 ml) good-quality vinegar

± 9 intestines or sausage casings

method

Combine the minced meat and pork fat. Work gently, otherwise the mixture will become stringy.

Roast the coriander in a hot, dry pan and then grind it finely. Sift to get rid of the husks and let it cool.

Combine all the spices and mix well with the meat mixture. Add the vinegar.

Leave the mixture for about 1 hour before filling the casings with the meat. The boerewors can either be eaten straight after making or stored in the refrigerator or freezer for later use.

To cook the boerewors, grill over the coals or fry in a pan until done to taste.

SOUP

During the seventeenth and eighteenth centuries, all the food for a main meal was placed on the table together. Salad was enjoyed first, after which meat, fish, vegetable and grain dishes followed. The position of soup in the order of dishes depended on the type of soup. Wheat soup would be eaten with the meat dish, while stock-based and sweet soups would be enjoyed last. Usually, fruit was eaten last to complete the meal.

At the beginning of the nineteenth century, soup started to replace lettuce as a starter. Different courses were also being served separately, in a specific order. Desserts were then served last with fruit and some of the original sweet soups became desserts.

The different types of soup served at the Cape during the seventeenth century can be divided into four groups:

- The Roman chef Apicius called the thick soup that developed during Roman times *potage*. The French absorbed this term for thick soup into their language. In the cookbook by Jannie de Villiers, *Namakwaland verhale-resepteboek* (1995), wheat soup is a good example of this type of soup. The wheat and meat were cooked together until both were very soft and the wheat had a sticky sauce. The meat was eaten first, followed by the wheat, which was enjoyed with milk or a helping of *kaiings* on top. Not all Cape soups were that thick, as the Cape vegetable soup on page 41. Vegetable soup often used meat stock, or was cooked with meat, poultry or game.

- In 1651, the French chef La Varenne was the first to create a recipe for stock and to prepare a *consommé* (clear soup) by using egg whites. The recipe for king's bread soup (see page 43), where the water used to cook vegetables or meat is poured over bread, is a forerunner of a clear soup.

- Recipes for sweet soups were possibly developed by the Italians. One of Scappi's recipes for sweet soup, in his *Opera* (1570) cookbook, mentions that fruit can be cooked with wine, sugar and cinnamon, and then served with bread in a small bowl. Granadilla (passion fruit) soup is another example of a sweet soup.

- *Swart suursop* (black sour soup) – a soup to which the blood of an animal was added to enrich and thicken it – is today unknown to Cape cooks, although it is still popular in some parts of Europe.

Barley soup

This economical dish has graced the menus of the poor for centuries. Today, the recipe for barley soup is so simplified that it usually only consists of ingredients such as meat bones, barley, onions, carrots, salt and pepper.

In old Cape Winelands cuisine, meat and fish were often used together in a recipe, as is the case with this soup.

SERVES: 6

ingredients

3 Tbsp (45 ml) olive oil

500 g lamb knuckle, sliced

2 onions, chopped

1 leek, sliced

2 stalks celery, chopped

2 carrots, chopped

just over ¾ cup (200 ml) pearl barley

zest and juice of 2 lemons

1 Tbsp (15 ml) chopped fresh dill

1 Tbsp (15 ml) chopped fresh oregano

2 Tbsp (30 ml) white wine vinegar

2 Tbsp (30 ml) fish sauce

2 Tbsp (30 ml) fruit chutney

8 cups (2 litres) lamb stock, or veal or vegetable stock (see recipes on pages 242–243)

½ cup (125 ml) marrow from beef marrowbones (optional)

1 tsp (5 ml) ground cinnamon

bouquet garni (bunch of herbs, bound with string or in a muslin bag, consisting of thyme, parsley, bay leaf, rosemary and fennel)

salt and freshly ground black pepper

chopped fresh dill and/or parsley, for garnishing

method

Heat a large saucepan and add the olive oil. Brown the lamb knuckle, and then remove with a slotted spoon and set aside.

Add the onions, leek, celery and carrots to the saucepan and sweat until soft (do not let it brown).

Return the lamb to the saucepan, along with the remaining ingredients (except the seasoning and garnish) and simmer for 1½–2 hours until the lamb is tender.

Remove and discard the bouquet garni, and season to taste with salt and black (or white) pepper. Sprinkle with freshly chopped dill and/or parsley just before serving.

Serve with crusty, homebaked bread.

Waterblommetjie
and sorrel soup

Waterblommetjies (Aponogeton distachyos), also known as Cape pondweed, are bulbous plants that thrive in slow-moving water or dams, particularly in the Western Cape. The flowers or stems of these plants are used in traditional soups and stews *(bredies)*.

Sorrel is a natural accompaniment to *waterblommetjies*. Cultivated or wild sorrel can be used. If using cultivated sorrel, first cut off the thick stems and finely chop up the leaves. If sorrel is not available, fresh lemon juice or vinegar can be used as a substitute.

During the reign of the Dutch East India Company, people were already aware of the health benefits and high Vitamin C content of sorrel, and sorrel soup was often served to scurvy sufferers. The soup was prepared by boiling sorrel stems and leaves together with a small amount of water in a pot over the fire until a thick porridge formed. It was then left to cool and later whisked with cold milk or buttermilk.

SERVES: 6

ingredients

1½ cups (375 ml) wild sorrel or
3 cups (3 x 250 ml) garden sorrel

3 Tbsp (45 ml) butter

2 onions, chopped

1 leek, chopped

1 stalk celery, sliced

zest and juice of 2 lemons

5 cups (5 x 250 ml) *waterblommetjies*

½ tsp (2.5 ml) grated nutmeg

4 cups (1 litre) chicken stock (see recipe on page 243)

4 cups (4 x 250 ml) spinach leaves (optional, for colour)

just over 1½ cups (400 ml) sour cream

1 tsp (5 ml) salt

¼ tsp (1 ml) ground white pepper

method

If using wild sorrel, rinse well to remove any sand. Place the sorrel and 2 cups (500 ml) water in a saucepan and bring to the boil. Stir until it forms a thick porridge (the sorrel stock). Remove from the heat and set aside. (If using garden sorrel, add at the same time as the spinach.)

Heat the butter in a separate, large saucepan and sweat the onions, leek, celery and lemon zest until softened, but not browned.

Add the sorrel stock, *waterblommetjies,* nutmeg and chicken stock and simmer for about 30 minutes until cooked.

Add the lemon juice, spinach (if using) and sour cream, and simmer for 5 minutes. Remove from the heat and blend until smooth. Season to taste with salt and pepper. Return to the stove to heat through, and then serve.

Corn and basil soup

Cape vegetable soup

Corn and basil soup

This is an old soup recipe, but it certainly would not seem out of place in any modern cookbook. The original recipe doesn't specify the herbs to be used and only refers to a 'bunch of herbs'. In this recipe we prefer to use basil, but you can replace it with herbs of your choice.

SERVES: 6

ingredients

2 Tbsp (30 ml) butter

2 onions, chopped

3 cups (3 x 250 ml) sweetcorn cut off the cob

6 cups (1.5 litres) chicken stock (see recipe on page 243)

1 cup (250 ml) fresh basil leaves

salt and freshly ground black pepper

method

Heat the butter in a large saucepan, add the onions and sweat until soft.

Add the sweetcorn and stock and simmer for 30 minutes. Remove from the heat, add the basil and blend using a hand-held blender or liquidiser. Pass through a fine sieve. Season to taste and serve hot or cold.

Cape vegetable soup

Vegetable soup has been part of Cape cuisine since the first Dutch settlers arrived here in 1652. Different vegetables, with or without meat or bacon, were used to prepare this soup. As was the custom 300 years ago when meat was omitted from soup, olive oil is used and the soup is thickened with finely ground nuts.

SERVES: 4

ingredients

1½ cups (375 ml) ground almonds

2 cloves garlic

2½ cups (625 ml) spiced vegetable stock (see recipe on page 242)

1 slice white bread, crusts removed

10 tsp (50 ml) sherry vinegar

¼ cup (60 ml) verjuice

½ cup (125 ml) olive oil (preferably not extra virgin, as it tends to give a bitter flavour)

salt and freshly ground black pepper

method

NOTE:

This soup also works well as a sauce for crayfish, prawns or crab.

Place all the ingredients, except the seasoning, in a large saucepan and bring to the boil. Blend until smooth and then season with salt and pepper to taste.

Can be served hot with croutons, or cold with a spoonful of chopped lettuce. Serve with a little olive oil drizzled over.

King's bread soup

The Dutch pastor and historian Gilles D.J. Schotel recorded the household practices performed during the seventeenth century in the Netherlands, and he described a soup he called *koningbroodsop* (king's bread soup). This soup was made from the stock of a *hutspot* (hotchpotch) and then served over bread. It was probably served in the same way at the Cape during Jan van Riebeeck's time.

Another version of this recipe, called *wittebroodsop* (white bread soup), was found in an old Cape cookbook. In this recipe the stock was mixed with milk and served over white bread.

The following recipe for king's bread soup consists of a traditional Cape bean soup and homemade bread. The savoury liquid is served over a slice of bread, while the beans and meat are then served separately.

SERVES: 12

ingredients

700 g beef shin or knuckle, cubed (reserve the bones)

salt and freshly ground black pepper

3 Tbsp (45 ml) olive oil

2 Tbsp (30 ml) butter

2 whole, smoked eisbein

1 bay leaf, crushed

1 tsp (5 ml) whole cloves

1 piece cassia bark

2 tsp (10 ml) whole allspice

2 onions, chopped

2 cloves garlic, chopped

1 leek, thinly sliced

1 large carrot, finely chopped or grated

2 cups (500 ml) good-quality red wine

8 cups (2 litres) lamb stock (see recipe on page 243)

1 cup (250 ml) dried kidney beans, soaked overnight in water

1 cup (250 ml) dried haricot beans, soaked overnight in water

juice and zest of 2 oranges

12 x 2 cm veal or beef marrowbones

12 deep-fried crumbed meatballs or chopped fresh parsley, for garnishing (optional)

method

Place the beef shin and bones into a large saucepan and cover with cold water. Bring to the boil, then remove from the heat immediately and strain off the water. Dry the meat well with paper towel. Season the shin well with salt and pepper.

Heat another large saucepan over high heat and add the olive oil and butter. Brown the beef shin and eisbein, and then remove and set aside. Reduce the heat.

Tie the bay leaf, cloves, cassia and allspice in a muslin bag, and add to the saucepan with the onions, garlic, leek and carrot and sweat gently until soft. Add the beef shin, eisbein and red wine and cook over high heat to reduce the wine by half.

Add the lamb stock, beans, orange juice and zest, cover the surface with parchment (baking) paper and simmer for 2–3 hours until the meat and beans are tender.

Preheat the oven to 200 °C (400 °F). Place the marrowbones in an oven pan and roast in the oven for 15 minutes, until browned and cooked. Set aside.

Take the soup off the heat. Pick the meat from the bones and return to the soup. Season to taste.

Use a large, flat soup plate. Place a mini potbread or slice of homemade bread in the middle, with a marrowbone on the side. Ladle the soup over and garnish with a crumbed meatball or chopped fresh parsley.

Lamb

and pomegranate soup

Pomegranates have been a source of food for humankind for thousands of years. In ancient Persia the pomegranate was revered and had many uses, including as a dye, a medicine, as well as in food and drink.

Pomegranates were planted in almost every Cape garden during the seventeenth and eighteenth centuries. As an aside, even rice was grown at the Cape during that time. Lady Anne Barnard claimed that the rice grown locally was of excellent quality, even better than the imported rice from Batavia.

SERVES: 6

Meatballs
ingredients

2 Tbsp (30 ml) ground coriander

1 small bunch spring onions, chopped

250 g lamb, minced

salt and freshly ground black pepper

method

Mix the coriander, spring onions and mince, and season with salt and pepper.

Roll the mince into tiny balls and set aside in the fridge until needed.

Soup
ingredients

⅓ cup (80 ml) long grain rice

⅓ cup (80 ml) green split peas

3 Tbsp (45 ml) olive oil

1 onion, chopped

½ tsp (2.5 ml) ground cinnamon

½ tsp (2.5 ml) turmeric

salt and freshly ground black pepper

8 cups (2 litres) chicken stock (see recipe on page 243)

1 small bunch parsley, chopped

60 g mint, chopped

6 Tbsp (90 ml) pomegranate syrup or substitute with 1 cup (250 ml) fresh pomegranate juice, reduced to 6 Tbsp (90 ml) and sweetened with 6 Tbsp (90 ml) sugar

salt and freshly ground black pepper

fresh pomegranate pips and chopped parsley, mint or coriander, for garnishing (optional)

method

Wash the rice and split peas and soak in water for 1 hour.

Heat the oil in a large saucepan and sauté the onion. Add the cinnamon, turmeric, and salt and pepper. Drain the rice and peas, and stir in. Pour over the stock and simmer for about 20 minutes until the rice and peas are cooked.

Drop the meatballs into the soup. Add the parsley and mint and simmer for 30 minutes.

Stir in the pomegranate syrup. (Add extra sugar to taste, if necessary.) Season with salt and pepper. Serve hot, sprinkled with fresh pomegranate pips and chopped parsley, mint or coriander.

Seafood soup

We can easily assume that fish soup was one of the first dishes served at the Cape, as people were often forced to turn to the harvests from the sea for survival because of initial food shortages, especially meat. The cooks at the Cape improvised and adapted their fish soup recipes according to the availability of ingredients and the seasons. Snoek head soup is one such adaptation and today it is still a favourite winter recipe.

Most of the old Cape fish soup recipes contained a mixture of seafood, a good-quality fish stock as a base, and herbs and spices. The soup was usually thickened with eggs and lemon juice, but sometimes seaweed was added to thicken the soup and enhance the flavour.

SERVES: 8

ingredients

1 Tbsp (15 ml) olive oil

1 Tbsp (15 ml) butter

1 onion, chopped

1 leek, finely sliced

1 stalk celery, finely sliced

1 clove garlic, pounded to a paste

1 tsp (5 ml) fresh root ginger, pounded to a paste

pinch of saffron (optional, and can be substituted with ½ tsp [2.5 ml] turmeric)

1 fresh red chilli, finely sliced

bouquet garni (thyme, bay leaf, parsley, fennel, chives, 2 crushed cardamom pods, 2 star anise)

zest and juice of 1 orange and 1 lemon, plus additional lemon juice

200 g Cape salmon, cubed

200 g white fish (such as hake or dorado)

200 g red fish (snapper or roman), cubed

just under 2½ cups (600 ml) fish stock (see recipe on page 244)

1 Tbsp (15 ml) ground dried seaweed (optional, but it adds a lovely taste)

¾ cup (190 ml) dry white wine

½ cup (125 ml) fresh cream

2 egg yolks

salt and freshly ground black pepper

300 g fresh black mussels, steamed (reserve the cooking liquid to add to the fish stock) or frozen mussels

chopped fresh parsley and dill, for garnishing (optional)

method

Heat the oil and butter in a large saucepan. Add the onion, leek, celery, garlic, ginger, saffron, chilli and bouquet garni and sweat until soft.

Add the citrus zest and juice and cook for 5 minutes.

Add all the fish, the fish stock, ground seaweed and wine and simmer for 15 minutes.

Add the cream and simmer for 5 minutes more. Remove and discard the bouquet garni.

Beat the egg yolks with a dash of lemon juice. Pour in 2 Tbsp (30 ml) of the hot soup and beat well. Pour the egg mixture into the saucepan and cook over very gentle heat until thick – do not let it boil. Season to taste.

Finally, just before serving, add the mussels (if using frozen, allow a minute or two to heat through) and garnish with chopped parsley and dill.

NOTE:

At the time of going to press, some of the fish listed above were on the SASSI (South African Sustainable Seafood Initiative) orange list, which means that increased demand could compromise a sustainable supply. Consider substituting from the green list; try panga, gurnard, angelfish or yellowtail instead. Or visit www.wwf.org.za/sassi for more information.

FISH AND SEAFOOD

During the Middle Ages, the freshness of fish was so important in the Netherlands that some ships had water tanks on board to keep the fish alive until they were sold. Dirk de Prins and Nest Mertens point out in *De Belgische Keuken* (1996) that unscrupulous people who sold rotten fish would have their property seized as punishment. At the Cape, Jan van Riebeeck also supported the practice of keeping fish fresh for as long as possible when he ordered a fishing boat to keep some fish alive in a trailing basket.

The first European pioneers at the Cape were very fortunate in being able to catch an abundance of fish in the seas around the Cape coast. When the weather prevented fishing, dried fish sent from the Netherlands to the Cape, as part of the rations, were still on offer.

Bountiful catches of steenbras, kingklip, harder (mullet), elf (shad), mackerel, snoek and hottentot (bronze bream) were recorded by Jan van Riebeeck. Octopus, crayfish, periwinkle, oysters, abalone and sea urchins supplemented their diet. Small shells were also collected and then boiled and scraped with a pin to get at the cooked delicacy inside. Hildagonda Duckitt's cookbook which appeared at the end of the nineteenth century also includes a recipe where these small shells were smashed and then boiled to prepare a stock for soup.

Today, oysters are very scarce in the seas around Cape Town, but from travellers' writings and the many old Cape recipes for this delicacy, it seems as if oysters used to be plentiful and popular. Oysters were used in various dishes, such as oyster cakes and pâté, as well as being filled, crumbed and even used in pies. During a trip inland in 1798, Lady Anne Barnard referred to a special treat – oysters – served by her host Jacob van Reenen on his farm between Swellendam and Heidelberg. Another oyster enthusiast, C. Louis Leipoldt, who supported the natural flavour of food above all else, strongly encouraged his readers to eat oysters without any unnecessary frills; just with a piece of bread and butter. However, he did record a recipe for chicken or fish with an oyster filling consisting of fresh oysters, breadcrumbs, marjoram, parsley, chilli, lemon juice, butter, nutmeg and egg yolk.

Oyster pâté

Curried fish

Oyster pâté

ingredients

1 onion, sliced

400 g oyster meat, juice reserved
(± 24 large, fresh oysters)

1 cup (250 ml) MCC or other
dry sparkling wine

2 sprigs fresh thyme

1 clove garlic, sliced

pinch of saffron

zest of 1 lemon

300 g butter, melted

5 eggs

1 tsp (5 ml) lemon juice

½ tsp (2.5 ml) salt

clarified butter

method

Place the onion, oyster juice, sparkling wine, thyme, garlic, saffron and lemon zest in a saucepan and cook slowly until only 1 tsp (5 ml) of syrupy liquid remains.

Add the oysters and warm through. Do not cook. Remove from the heat.

Melt the butter and keep warm.

Place the oyster and onion mixture in a blender with the eggs and half the melted butter. Add the lemon juice and salt and blend until smooth.

Pass through a fine sieve and beat in the rest of the warm butter.

Place in desired moulds in a *bain marie* (water bath), cover the tray with foil and bake at 150 °C (300 °F) for 20–40 minutes until set. Leave to cool.

Pour clarified butter on the surface of the pâté and refrigerate.

Serve with onion marmalade and toasted sourdough bread, or any other bread of your choice.

NOTE:

MCC, or Méthode Cap Classique, is South African sparkling wine made according to the traditional French method for making champagne.

Oyster
and marrow pies

During Jan van Riebeeck's time at the Cape, cooking with marrow as a replacement for butter, fat or oil wasn't seen as the luxury it is today; in fact, it was a favoured ingredient. Serve these pies as a starter for a gourmet dinner, or make bite-sized pies and serve as canapés.

MAKES: 12–15 small pies

ingredients

1 Tbsp (15 ml) butter

1 onion, chopped

1 clove garlic, chopped

1 tsp (5 ml) smoked sweet paprika (optional)

pinch of cayenne pepper

¼ tsp (1 ml) chopped fresh ginger

½ cup (125 ml) dry white wine

½ cup (125 ml) sherry

1 tsp (5 ml) fish sauce

½ cup (125 ml) currants

1½ cups (375 ml) shucked oysters, juice reserved

½ cup (125 ml) veal marrow (roasted, removed from bone and diced)

zest of 1 lemon

1 cup (250 ml) fish stock (see recipe on page 244)

2½ tsp (12.5 ml) cornflour or potato flour

1 Tbsp (15 ml) chopped fresh parsley

600 g flaky pastry, rolled 4 mm thick and cut into 8 cm circles (see recipe on page 253)

1 egg, beaten with 1 tsp (5 ml) water, for brushing pastry

method

Preheat the oven to 220 °C (425 °F).

Heat a frying pan, brown the butter and add the onion, garlic, spices and ginger and reduce the heat to low. Sweat until the onion is tender.

Add the white wine, sherry and fish sauce and cook until syrupy.

Add the currants, oysters and their juice, marrow, lemon zest and fish stock and bring to a boil. Reduce the heat to low and simmer for 5 minutes.

Slake the cornflour or potato flour with 1 tsp (5 ml) cold water, add to the saucepan and simmer for 5 minutes until thick. Leave to cool and then add the parsley.

Brush the surface of each pastry square with the egg wash. Place two heaped tablespoons of filling in the centre, fold the pastry over and secure the edges with a pinch.

Brush with egg wash and bake for about 25 minutes until golden.

Pickled fish

In some of the old cookbooks, the terms 'curried fish' and 'pickled fish' were used indiscriminately, causing confusion as to the ingredients used. Generally, however, pickled fish referred to a recipe where the fish was cooked in flavoured vinegar, without the addition of saffron or turmeric.

In this mouthwatering recipe, raisins and a boiled vinegar-and-spice mixture are used to prepare this delectable dish.

SERVES: 6

ingredients

4 Tbsp (60 ml) coarse sea salt

1.2 kg white fish fillets

1 red onion, sliced

zest of 1 lemon

1 cup (250 ml) cake flour

1 tsp (5 ml) smoked paprika (optional)

pinch of salt

vegetable oil, for frying

1¼ cups (300 ml) white wine vinegar

1¼ cups (300 ml) dry white wine

5 sprigs fresh marjoram

6 cloves garlic, sliced

1 Tbsp (15 ml) capers

1 Tbsp (15 ml) seedless raisins

olive oil, for drizzling

method

Salt the fish and leave to stand for 30 minutes. Rinse and pat dry with paper towel.

Scatter half the onion and the lemon zest in a glassware dish large enough to fit all the fish in a single layer.

Mix the flour, paprika and a pinch of salt. Dredge the fish through the flour and fry in oil for a few minutes until cooked.

Add the vinegar, wine, marjoram and garlic to a small saucepan and bring to the boil.

Place the fish on top of the onion slices in the dish, top with the remaining onion slices and pour the hot vinegar mixture over.

Sprinkle with the capers and raisins. Pour the olive oil over, cover and refrigerate for a few days, preferably a week, before serving with homemade bread as a starter or as a main course with a crisp garden salad.

Cape fish 'spread'

This recipe comes from Mary Sanderson's handwritten eighteenth-century cookbook. It is interesting to note that spreads were already part of Cape cuisine by the seventeenth century.

SERVES: 4

ingredients

1 sprig fresh marjoram

1 sprig fresh parsley

2 sprigs fresh thyme

2 bay leaves

2 Tbsp (30 ml) butter

4 harders (mullet) or ½ snoek, scaled, gutted and fins removed

salt and freshly ground black pepper

¼ tsp (1 ml) ground mace or grated nutmeg

pinch of ground cloves

3 Tbsp (45 ml) clarified butter

2 anchovy fillets, finely chopped

method

Preheat the oven to 180 °C (350 °F).

Chop the herbs and add to the butter in a saucepan. Melt the butter and pour over the fish in a casserole dish.

Season the fish with salt and pepper, cover with parchment (baking) paper and bake for about 30 minutes until cooked.

Pick the fish from the bones and flake. Set aside.

Mix the mace or nutmeg, cloves, half the clarified butter, the anchovies and the flaked fish together and pound to a paste. Scoop into a sterilised dish.

Pour the remaining clarified butter over the spread to cover the surface and then refrigerate.

Serve with flat bread or Melba toast and onion relish.

Braised snoek

Gesmoorde (braised) snoek is an inexpensive, traditional dish that makes a regular appearance at the table during the cold Cape winters. The most well-known method for preparing this dish is as follows: Sauté onions in lots of butter together with pepper, salt, fresh ginger, lemon zest and juice, and a pinch of fresh chilli. Then add cooked flaked fish (fresh, salted or smoked) and braise slowly until cooked. Traditionally potatoes were added and some modern cooks prefer to add fresh tomatoes with the pips and skins removed.

The recipe given below is an interesting adaptation of a braised snoek recipe from the nineteenth century. Snoek is recommended as the main ingredient, but any firm fish will do. Adding eggs to thicken and enrich the sauce is also an unusual variation on the traditional recipe.

The original recipe recommends that a glass of sherry be poured over the dish at the end, but we replaced the sherry with Chardonnay.

SERVES: 6 starter portions or 4 main portions

ingredients

1 Tbsp (15 ml) butter

1 kg salted snoek, soaked in milk for 12 hours (if using fresh or smoked snoek instead, you do not need to soak it)

2 onions, thinly sliced

½ tsp (2.5 ml) grated nutmeg

1 tsp (5 ml) ground allspice

¼ tsp (1 ml) ground cloves

½ tsp (2.5 ml) finely chopped fresh root ginger

2 cups (500 ml) fish stock (see recipe on page 244)

¾ cup (190 ml) Chardonnay or other dry white wine

1 bay leaf

1 tsp (5 ml) lemon zest

salt and ground white pepper

2 egg yolks

4 tsp (20 ml) lemon juice

2 Tbsp (30 ml) chopped fresh parsley, fennel or dill, for garnishing

method

Heat a frying pan, brown the butter and add the snoek. Cook the snoek over moderate heat until golden brown. Remove from the pan, let it cool and flake the fish from the bones. Discard the bones and skin.

Add the onions, nutmeg, allspice, cloves and ginger to the pan and sauté until the onions are tender. Strain off any excess butter.

Add the fish stock, wine, flaked snoek, bay leaf and lemon zest, and place parchment (baking) paper on the surface to prevent too much liquid evaporating. Season with salt and white pepper, and simmer over low heat for 20–30 minutes. Remove from the heat and strain the sauce into a saucepan, leaving the solid ingredients in the frying pan.

Beat the egg yolks and lemon juice together and add half the strained sauce. Mix through well and pour back into the saucepan. Cook over low heat until the sauce coats the back of a spoon. Add another egg if the sauce is too thin.

Pour the sauce over the snoek and heat through gently. Garnish with chopped parsley, fennel or dill and serve with sliced bread or rolls, dried apricot slices and a tomato salsa.

Fish larded
with anchovy

Larding — when pieces of fat are inserted into a cut of meat with a needle or sharp object to provide extra moisture and flavour — is usually associated with meat, especially venison. The fat can be replaced with any other ingredient, as long as it adds moisture to make the dish more succulent.

An interesting Dutch recipe from the sixteenth century mentions the larding of fish with salted anchovy before it is grilled over the coals. This flavourful dish is served with a sauce consisting of verjuice and egg. Verjuice (unfermented fruit juice) has been in use since long before the Dutch established the refreshment station at the Cape and can be made from any unripe fruit, or even sorrel. Because the taste is less tart than vinegar, it makes for a piquant accompaniment to fish.

In general, the taste of fresh fish should not be obliterated by strong or spicy flavours, but this recipe can be useful when using larger, dry fish.

SERVES: 4

FISH
ingredients

4 firm fish fillets with skin (yellowtail or panga are good choices)

coarse sea salt and freshly ground black pepper

4 Tbsp (60 ml) chopped sorrel

zest and juice of 1 lemon

4 Tbsp (60 ml) chopped fresh parsley

pinch of rosemary or *kapokbos* (wild rosemary), chopped

2 cloves garlic

1 tsp (5 ml) chopped fresh root ginger

pinch of ground cinnamon

pinch of grated nutmeg

12 small anchovy fillets, soaked in milk to get rid of excess salt

2 Tbsp (30 ml) olive oil

method

Preheat the oven to 180 °C (350 °F).

Score the skin of the fish by making 4 mm incisions into the flesh (three incisions per fillet).

Place the coarse salt, pepper, sorrel, lemon zest, parsley, rosemary or *kapokbos*, garlic and ginger in a mortar and grind to a coarse paste. Add the spices and mix through.

Press 1 anchovy fillet into each of the incisions made, followed by ¼ tsp (1 ml) of the paste. Use the back of a knife and press the paste into the incisions.

Heat a frying pan and add olive oil.

Dry the skin of the fish as much as possible using paper towel, sprinkle with sea salt and add the fish to the pan, skin side down. Cook the fish for 3–4 minutes until the skin is golden brown. Turn the fish over and place in the oven for 5 minutes. Remove the fish and pour the lemon juice over.

Serve with Verjuice Butter Sauce.

VERJUICE BUTTER SAUCE
ingredients

1½ cups (375 ml) verjuice

1 tsp (5 ml) cornflour

100 g butter

salt and freshly ground black pepper

method

Pour the verjuice into a small saucepan and bring to the boil.

Mix the cornflour with 2 tsp (10 ml) cold water and add to the verjuice. Cook for 3 minutes, stirring.

Place the butter in a frying pan and heat until golden brown.

Beat the butter into the hot sauce and season to taste. Serve immediately, or keep warm, covered with parchment (baking) paper, until ready to serve.

fish and seafood

Cape bokkom salad

According to G.D.J. Schotel, *bokkom* (dried harder or mullet) is a Dutch word used during the seventeenth century to refer to smoked as well as dried herring. Fish with the head, stomach and scales intact were stacked in layers with salt in-between and left for 24 hours, whereafter they were hung up to dry out. Various fish species were dried in this way, of which harder (mullet) was the most popular.

 Many people from other parts of South Africa and overseas first get to know the unusual taste of *bokkoms* while visiting the Cape. Those who have a good teacher to show them how to clean a *bokkom* easily, will soon be asking for more of this delicacy. It makes for an appetising starter when half-dried and quickly grilled over the coals.

 Jan van Riebeeck's granddaughter wrote to her mother in Batavia in 1710 and mentioned that she prepared *bokkoms* with parsley butter. She was probably referring to half-dried *bokkoms* that were lightly pan-fried.

SERVES: 3

DRESSING
ingredients

2 egg yolks

1 tsp (5 ml) chopped garlic (wild garlic if possible)

1 tsp (5 ml) lemon juice

1 cup (250 ml) finely grated matured pecorino cheese

pinch of salt

1 tsp (5 ml) Dijon mustard

1 tsp (5 ml) fresh cream

2 anchovy fillets, pounded to a paste

1¼ cups (300 ml) oil (grapeseed oil or a mild olive oil blend)

¼ cup (60 ml) fish stock (see recipe on page 244) or tomato juice

salt and freshly ground black pepper

method

Place the egg yolks, garlic, lemon juice, pecorino, salt, mustard, cream and anchovy paste in a bowl. Whisk and add the oil a few drops at a time until all is emulsified.

Add the stock or juice a little at a time until the dressing achieves the desired thickness. Season with salt and pepper to taste.

SALAD
ingredients

200 g mixed lettuce

1 bokkom fillet, cut into very fine strips

¼ cup (60 ml) sun-dried tomatoes

¼ cup (60 ml) shaved pecorino cheese

¼ cup (60 ml) flaked almonds, toasted

12 semi hard-boiled quail's eggs, halved

50 g dried apricots, chopped

¼ cup (60 ml) dressing (see left)

¼ cup (60 ml) croutons

method

Place the lettuce in a bowl. Add the rest of the ingredients, except the croutons, and toss using your hands. Rub the dressing over the leaves. Sprinkle the croutons over the top and serve.

Franschhoek trout
with red wine sauce

Fish with a red wine sauce was popular fare at the Cape and in Europe during the seventeenth and eighteenth centuries. Modern variations include tomatoes, which only became popular in Europe during the nineteenth century and, as such, our recipe follows the older method, leaving out the tomatoes.

SERVES: 2

FISH
ingredients

1 freshwater trout (or 1 whole eel), filleted and skinned

olive oil, for frying

½ cup (125 ml) pumpkin seeds

½ cup (125 ml) chopped almonds

method

Preheat the oven to 220 °C (425 °F).

Sear the fish in hot olive oil in a frying pan.

Mix the seeds and nuts together and sprinkle over the fish. Bake in the oven for 5 minutes for medium-rare or 10 minutes for well done.

SAUCE
ingredients

¼ cup (60 ml) chopped mixed field mushrooms or brown mushrooms

1 onion, chopped

¼ tsp (1 ml) chopped garlic

1 Tbsp (15 ml) picked fresh thyme

1½ cups (375 ml) good-quality red wine

½ cup (125 ml) medium sherry

1 cup (250 ml) strong mushroom stock (see recipe on page 245)

1 cup (250 ml) fish stock (see recipe on page 244)

1 tsp (5 ml) butter

lemon juice to taste

1 Tbsp (15 ml) finely chopped fresh parsley

salt and freshly ground black pepper

method

Heat a frying pan and cook the mushrooms over high heat until golden brown. Reduce the heat and add the onion, garlic and thyme. Sweat until soft.

Add the red wine and sherry and cook to a glaze.

Add the mushroom and fish stocks and reduce by three-quarters until thickened.

Remove from the heat and beat in the butter. Add a squeeze of lemon juice and the parsley. Season to taste.

Place the trout fillets on two dinner plates and pour the sauce over (or serve separately).

Serve with a field mushroom and corn stir-fry.

Lightly curried mussels
on potato pancakes

No recipes for the preparation of mussels could be traced in old Cape cookbooks. This could possibly be due to the simplicity of most mussel recipes, or because indigenous Cape black mussels (*Choromytilus meridionalis*) were not seen as an appetising delicacy. *Mytilus galloprovincialis*, the species that is now harvested locally, was only brought to the Cape much later via ships from abroad. C. Louis Leipoldt writes that the blue-and-white mussels were the most popular. He prepared them using simple ingredients, as we still do today, but he added a dash of brandy for a typical Cape flavour.

This recipe is adapted from an old fifteenth-century Dutch cookbook titled *Wel ende edelike spijse*.

SERVES: 6 as a starter

POTATO PANCAKE BATTER
(for 18 small pancakes)
ingredients

250 g cooked mashed potatoes

1½ tsp (7.5 ml) ground coriander

¼ tsp (1 ml) ground cumin

1 tsp (5 ml) chopped fresh parsley

pinch of freshly ground black pepper

¼ tsp (1 ml) salt

2 eggs

1 egg yolk

1 Tbsp (15 ml) sour cream or cream cheese

3 Tbsp (45 ml) buckwheat or cake flour

1 Tbsp (15 ml) olive oil

CURRIED MUSSELS
ingredients

1 tsp (5 ml) olive oil

1 onion, sliced

1 tsp (5 ml) coriander seeds

½ tsp (2.5 ml) mustard seeds

pinch of saffron

1 lemon leaf

1 tsp (5 ml) lemon zest

1 clove garlic, sliced

1 tsp (5 ml) chopped fresh root ginger

2 tsp (10 ml) curry mix 1 (see recipe on page 248)

1 cup (250 ml) fish stock (see recipe on page 244)

1 cup (250 ml) Chardonnay or other dry white wine

18 fresh black mussels, beards removed and rinsed (discard any that are open), or frozen mussels

1 cup (250 ml) fresh cream

1 tsp (5 ml) chopped fresh dill

salt and freshly ground black pepper

sorrel, for garnishing

method

Beat the mash, spices, parsley, seasoning, eggs, egg yolk and sour cream or cream cheese until well mixed. Fold in the flour and leave to rest for 1 hour in the refrigerator.

Heat a non-stick or blini pan and add a little of the olive oil (too much oil will cause the pancake to form a hard crust). Scoop 1 Tbsp (15 ml) of pancake batter into the pan and flatten slightly. The pancakes must be about 6 mm thick and 3 cm in diameter.

Fry until light brown and gently flip. The pancakes must be light, thin and not too firm. Repeat until all the batter is used up.

method

Heat a saucepan and add the olive oil. Add the onion, coriander and mustard seeds, saffron, lemon leaf and zest, garlic and ginger. Sweat until soft.

Add the curry mix and cook for 1 minute. Add the fish stock and wine and bring to the boil.

Heat a frying pan with a tight-fitting lid until very hot. Add the mussels and the onion and stock mixture and place the lid on top. Steam for a few minutes until the mussels are open (discard any that have not opened).

Strain the sauce through a sieve, and then place the sauce back on the heat and reduce until thick. Add the cream and cook to desired consistency. Add the dill and season to taste.

Place the mussels back in the sauce and heat through. Create a stack of three mussels and three pancakes per portion, and place on a plate. Drizzle the sauce over and around the mussels and garnish with sorrel.

Salt fish
and sweet potato stew

Lichtenstein, a German visitor to the Cape, wrote in 1803 about a typical South African national dish he ate while visiting the Hex River Valley. He described this tantalising meal as consisting of salt fish, *kalbas* (calabash pumpkin) and finely sliced onions. For this recipe the calabash pumpkin is replaced with sweet potato, which is more readily available.

SERVES: 4

FISH
ingredients

500 g fleshy white fish, filleted
(yellowtail is a good choice)

1 cup (250 ml) coarse sea salt

method

Cut the fish into 100 g pieces and dredge in the salt. Place in a glass container and pack tightly with the remaining salt. Set aside in the refrigerator for at least 48 hours.

Soak in milk overnight before using to remove the excess salt. (The salt fish can be substituted with flaked, salted snoek.)

SWEET POTATO STEW
ingredients

2 Tbsp (30 ml) olive oil

2 onions, chopped

2 cloves garlic, chopped

1 Tbsp (15 ml) chopped fresh root ginger

2 cinnamon sticks

1 tsp (5 ml) ground cumin

1 tsp (5 ml) ground coriander

1 tsp (5 ml) salt (omit if the fish is still salty after soaking)

1 cup (250 ml) fish stock (see recipe on page 244)

¼ cup (60 ml) white wine vinegar

pinch of saffron

½ cup (125 ml) brown sugar

500 g sweet potato, peeled and diced, or calabash pumpkin or maranka

½ cup (125 ml) seedless raisins

½ cup (125 ml) whole almonds

method

Preheat the oven to 180 °C (350 °F).

Heat a frying pan, add the olive oil and sweat the onions, garlic and ginger until tender. Add the spices and salt (if using) and fry for 1 minute until fragrant.

Add the fish stock, vinegar, saffron and sugar and bring to the boil.

Layer the sweet potato and raisins in a casserole dish, top with the fish and pour the hot contents of the pan over.

Sprinkle the almonds over the top, fit the lid and place in the oven for about 20 minutes until the sweet potato is tender. Serve with rice and Cucumber and Bean Sambal (see page 172).

NOTE:

If using pumpkin, especially the greener varieties, use less fish stock, as the pumpkin draws a lot of water during the cooking process.

CURRY

Before commercial curry powder was available at the Cape, every cook had his or her own recipe for curry mix. In the oldest Dutch, Flemish and Cape recipe manuscripts, many curry recipes were documented. We chose three of these, which we adapted only slightly for use by the modern cook.

The oldest recipe comes from Thomas van der Noot's recipe book of 1510. In his book, curry recipes such as pig's tripe and curried fish with saffron were included. He did not give exact measurements, but merely listed the ingredients.

The second recipe was found in a handwritten cookbook by Mary Sanderson. The inscription on the yellowed pages of this cookbook reads '1770'.

The last recipe was found in a copy of Wilhelmina Mostert's cookbook (ca. mid-1800s), which listed the recipes in her neat handwriting, with references to where they originated.

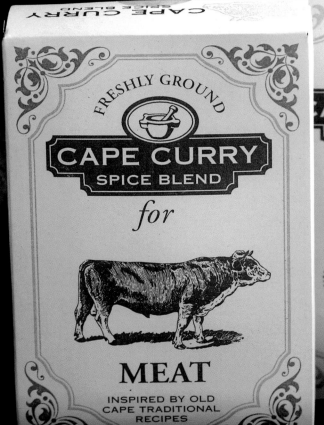

FRESHLY GROUND

CAPE CURRY

SPICE BLEND

for

MEAT

INSPIRED BY OLD
CAPE TRADITIONAL
RECIPES

FRESHLY GRO...

CAPE C...

SPICE BLE...

for

FISH

INSPIRED BY OL...
CAPE TRADITION...
RECIPES

FRESHLY GROUND

CAPE CURRY

SPICE BLEND

for

POULTRY
& VEGETABLES

INSPIRED BY OLD
CAPE TRADITIONAL
RECIPES

MILD & AROMATIC

85

Curry mixes

Thomas van der Noot's 1510 curry mix for fish

MAKES: ± 2 kg

ingredients

200 g cardamom pods

400 g ground ginger

100 g whole cloves

900 g turmeric (original recipe used saffron)

300 g ground cinnamon

200 g dried galangal

method

Pound all the ingredients together using a pestle and mortar or spice grinder.

Can be stored in an airtight container for no longer than 2 months.

MAKES: ± 500 g

Mary Sanderson's 1770 curry mix

ingredients

90 g coriander seeds

90 g cumin seeds

90 g ground ginger

30 g black peppercorns

180 g turmeric

30 g cayenne pepper

pinch of saffron

2 cardamom pods

1 cinnamon stick

method

Pound all the ingredients together using a pestle and mortar or spice grinder.

This mix can be used for beef, lamb or chicken curries, and can be stored in an airtight container for no longer than 2 months.

Wilhelmina Mostert's 1847 curry mix (*om kerrie kruiden te maken*)

MAKES: ± 1 kg

ingredients

125 g ground ginger

350 g turmeric

75 g ground cumin

500 g coriander seeds, toasted

6 orange leaves (can substitute with 2 bay leaves)

½-piece whole nutmeg

10 whole cloves

pinch of chilli powder

method

Pound all the ingredients together using a pestle and mortar or spice grinder.

A good mix for beef, lamb or chicken, it can be stored in an airtight container for no longer than 2 months.

NOTE:

Three more curry mixtures on page 248

Curried fish

The sauce for curried fish contains, among other spices, saffron or turmeric, which gives the curry flavour and its characteristic yellow colour. The curry powders available in shops today usually all contain turmeric, which is far less expensive than the saffron that was predominantly used in the old Cape recipes.

SERVES: 5

ingredients

sunflower oil, for frying

1 kg hake, cut into 5 x 200 g portions

salt and freshly ground black pepper

5 medium onions, cut into rings

½ cup (125 ml) sugar

1 Tbsp (15 ml) curry mix 1
(see recipe on page 248)

2 tsp (10 ml) turmeric

½ tsp (2.5 ml) coriander
seeds, toasted

2 star anise

2 cinnamon sticks

1 large knob fresh root
ginger, peeled and chopped

2 whole allspice

¼ cup (60 ml) apricot jam

3 cups (750 ml) vinegar

1 cup (250 ml) water

4 orange or bay leaves

method

Heat the oil in a large frying pan. Season the hake with salt and pepper and fry until cooked. Set aside.

Place the rest of the ingredients in a large saucepan, bring to the boil and simmer together for 25 minutes.

Layer the fish in a glass or ceramic dish (with a lid) and pour the warm sauce over. Let it cool. Cover the dish with the lid and place in the refrigerator overnight before serving.

Photograph on page 52

curry

Lentil sambal

Cape seafood curry

Cucumber and bean sambal

Beetroot and horseradish sambal

Chicken curry

Cape lamb curry

Chicken curry

Some of the documented variations of this sixteenth-century curry recipe contained raisins or dried figs, and freshwater fish such as carp or eel were often used instead of chicken. For this recipe, typical South African ingredients — dried apricots and raisins — are used. Although coconut cream was not used in the original, it is included in our contemporary recipe — the popular way in which chicken curry is served in the Cape Winelands today.

SERVES: 4-6

ingredients

3 Tbsp (45 ml) butter

1 whole chicken, deboned and cut into portions

1 onion, chopped

2 sour apples, cored and chopped

1 cup (250 ml) dried apricots, soaked in water and sliced

½ cup (125 ml) seedless raisins

1 Tbsp (15 ml) sugar

1 Tbsp (15 ml) salt

1 clove garlic, chopped

1 tsp (5 ml) tamarind paste dissolved in 1 cup (250 ml) water

3 Tbsp (45 ml) curry mix 2 (see recipe on page 248)

3 Tbsp (45 ml) white wine vinegar

½ cup (125 ml) coconut cream

1 Tbsp (15 ml) chopped fresh sage or fresh coriander leaves

method

Heat a stovetop casserole dish or large saucepan. Brown the butter and add the chicken pieces. Cook on all sides until golden brown. Remove from the pan and set aside.

Add the onion to the saucepan and cook for 5 minutes. Add the apples, apricots, raisins and sugar and let it caramelise.

Add the salt, garlic, tamarind water, curry mix and vinegar and dissolve in the caramel.

Add the chicken pieces and cover with a lid. Cook over low heat for 1 hour. (If the sauce reduces while cooking the chicken, add some chicken stock or water to top up.)

Remove the lid, add the coconut cream and sage or coriander and increase the heat to reduce the sauce to the desired consistency.

Serve with Cape fruit chutney and rice.

Cape seafood curry

SEAFOOD ingredients

300 g yellowtail, cubed

300 g red roman, cubed

300 g butterfish, cubed

4 fish roe

1 Tbsp (15 ml) butter

30 black mussels, steamed in
a little white wine and water
until opened, stock reserved

method

Pan-fry the fish and roe in a little butter until
browned and just cooked. Set aside and keep
warm while making the sauce.

NOTE:

At the time of going to print, some of the fish
listed above were on the SASSI (South African
Sustainable Seafood Initiative) orange list,
which means that increased demand could
compromise a sustainable supply. Consider
substituting from the green list; try panga,
gurnard, dorado, angelfish or yellowtail
instead. Or visit www.wwf.org.za/sassi for
more information.

CURRY SAUCE ingredients

1 Tbsp (15 ml) olive oil

1 large red onion, chopped

4 stalks celery, chopped

4 cloves garlic, chopped

½ fresh red chilli, chopped

3 Tbsp (45 ml) curry mix 2 (see recipe on page 248)

1 Tbsp (15 ml) lemon juice

2 tsp (10 ml) fish sauce

8 cups (2 litres) fish stock (see recipe
on page 244; add reserved liquid
from steamed mussels)

pinch of saffron

1 can (400 ml) coconut cream

just over ½ cup (150 ml) buttermilk

salt and freshly ground black pepper

½ cup (125 ml) fresh basil, chopped

method

Heat the olive oil in a large saucepan and sauté the onion,
celery, garlic and chilli. Add the curry mix and sauté for
3 minutes.

Add the lemon juice, fish sauce, stock, saffron and coconut
cream and reduce until slightly thickened.

Add the fish, roe and mussels, and then add the buttermilk.
Heat through and season to taste with salt and pepper.

Ladle into a deep serving dish. Serve sprinkled with chopped
basil, with crusty bread on the side to soak up the sauce, or
basmati rice and a tomato and cucumber sambal.

Photograph on page 80

Cape lamb curry

In the old Cape recipes ginger is used together with pepper, as in this recipe. The custom originates from the time when pepper was so expensive that impoverished cooks opted for ginger to flavour their curry dishes.

SERVES: 4–6

ingredients

1 tsp (5 ml) freshly ground black pepper

½ tsp (2.5 ml) ground ginger

1 tsp (5 ml) salt

2 Tbsp (30 ml) cake flour

400 g lamb rib or breast, cubed

300 g lamb shoulder, cubed

5 Tbsp (75 ml) lamb's tail fat or oil

1 onion, chopped

1 clove garlic, chopped

1 bulb fennel, chopped

zest and juice of 1 lemon

1 Tbsp (15 ml) chopped dried orange peel

4 Tbsp (60 ml) curry mix 3 (see recipe on page 248)

1 cup (250 ml) tamarind water (see Chicken Curry recipe on page 81) or ¼ cup (60 ml) wine vinegar

1 Tbsp (15 ml) vinegar

2 cups (500 ml) buttermilk

4 cups (1 litre) lamb stock

1 cup (250 ml) baby carrots

1 cup (250 ml) baby turnips

1 tsp (5 ml) chopped fresh rosemary

¼ cup (60 ml) fresh basil, chopped

¼ cup (60 ml) whole almonds, blanched

method

Preheat the oven to 160 °C (325 °F).

Mix the dry ingredients together and lightly coat the lamb. Heat 4 Tbsp (60 ml) tail fat or oil in a large frying pan and fry the meat in small batches until golden brown. Set aside.

Use a large, heavy-based casserole dish with a tight-fitting lid that can also be used on the stovetop, and brown the onion lightly in the remaining tail fat or oil.

Add the garlic, fennel, lemon juice and zest, orange peel, curry mix, tamarind water or wine vinegar and vinegar. Bring to the boil and add the buttermilk. Cover with the lid and place in the oven for 1½–2 hours.

Remove the dish from the oven and add the carrots, turnips, herbs and almonds. Simmer slowly, uncovered, over low heat for about 30 minutes until the sauce has thickened and the vegetables are tender. Season to taste with salt and pepper.

Serve with rice and sambals.

Photograph on page 80

Cucumber salad

Bobotie

The oldest known bobotie (curried minced meat) recipe originated with Apicius, who cooked for the wealthy during the reign of the Roman Empire. This sweet-and-sour dish was baked with the characteristic egg custard on top and meat, fish, vegetables, nuts, herbs and spices were added to the recipe.

The first bobotie made at the Cape probably followed the old Roman recipe due to a shortage of meat, fish and vegetables. Fortunately the abundance of sea birds provided a steady supply of eggs. When meat became more readily available later on, bobotie was prepared with only meat (always cooked), nuts and, sometimes, dried fruit. A fish bobotie was also made, and the egg custard was used over vegetable dishes, as is still the custom in the Balkans today.

The traditional recipe given below calls for cooked meat, as cooks used to do in days gone by. Today the 1 kg cooked meat can be substituted with 1.3 kg raw mutton or beef mince. This will, however, change the sequence in the method of the recipe. If using raw mince, fry the onions, add the spices and sauté for 3 minutes, and then add the mince with the rest of the ingredients.

SERVES: 6–8

MEAT MIXTURE
ingredients

2 Tbsp (30 ml) sunflower oil

2 onions, chopped

1 kg cooked and minced mutton or beef

1 thick slice bread

1 cup (250 ml) beef or mutton stock (see recipe on page 243)

1 egg

1 cup (250 ml) milk

2½ Tbsp (37.5 ml) curry mix 3 (see recipe on page 248)

1 tsp (5 ml) turmeric

¼ cup (60 ml) apricot jam

2 tsp (10 ml) salt (less if meat was already salted when cooked)

¼ tsp (1 ml) cayenne pepper

3 Tbsp (45 ml) wine vinegar

½ cup (125 ml) seedless raisins

1 Tbsp (15 ml) chopped fresh root ginger, or more to taste

1 pkt (100 g) blanched and ground almonds

EGG CUSTARD
ingredients

3 fresh lemon or bay leaves

2 eggs

1½ cups (375 ml) milk

method

Preheat the oven to 180 °C (350 °F) and grease an ovenproof dish.

Heat the oil in a large saucepan and sauté the onions until cooked and slightly browned. Add the meat.

Soak the bread in the meat stock, and then mash with a fork. Whisk the egg and milk together and add to bread. Add this to the meat and onion mixture and bring slowly to boiling point.

Mix the rest of the ingredients together and add to the meat mixture.

Ladle the meat into the ovenproof dish. Smooth the top neatly so that when you pour the egg custard on top it can distribute evenly. (At this stage the meat can be frozen, if using a freezer-safe dish. Defrost in a medium oven, before pouring over the custard.)

Bake for 30 minutes.

Remove the dish from the oven. Roll the lemon or bay leaves into cone shapes and press into the meat mixture. Beat the eggs and milk together, pour over the bobotie and place the dish back into the oven. Bake until the custard is set and golden brown, about 20 minutes.

Serve with rice and sambals.

Mussel bobotie
with pickles

ingredients

1 Tbsp (15 ml) butter

2 Tbsp (30 ml) olive oil

1 clove garlic, chopped

1 onion, chopped

1 tsp (5 ml) chopped fresh
root ginger

4 Tbsp (60 ml) curry mix 1
(see recipe on page 248)

2 Tbsp (30 ml) brown sugar

3 Tbsp (45 ml) white wine vinegar

500 g mussel meat, minced

1 cup (250 ml) fresh breadcrumbs,
soaked in 1 cup (250 ml) milk

salt and freshly ground
black pepper

3 Tbsp (45 ml) seedless raisins

1 Tbsp (15 ml) chopped
fresh parsley

zest and juice of 1 lemon

½ cup (125 ml) blanched
almonds, chopped

7 eggs

1 lemon leaf

7 Tbsp (105 ml) milk

1½ cups (375 ml) cream cheese
or substitute with Greek yoghurt

method

Preheat the oven to 180 °C (350 °F).

Heat a large frying pan and melt the butter. Add the olive oil and sauté the
garlic, onion and ginger. Add the curry mix and fry for 2 minutes.

Add the brown sugar and caramelise, and then deglaze with the vinegar.

Mix the mussel meat with the soaked breadcrumbs. Add the onion mixture
to the mussel meat and season well.

Add the raisins, parsley, lemon zest and juice and almonds and mix well.

Beat 2 of the eggs and add to the mussel mixture. Pour into a buttered
ovenproof dish and top with the lemon leaf. Bake for 30 minutes.

Beat the remaining 5 eggs with the milk and cream cheese or yoghurt and
season well. Remove the dish from the oven and pour the egg mixture over
the top.

Return the dish to the oven and bake for about 40 minutes until the custard
is firm to the touch.

Serve with rice and fruit pickle.

Poultry, Meat, Game and Offal

When Jan van Riebeeck established a refreshment station at the Cape in 1652 to provide passing ships with fresh produce, the expectation was that fresh meat would be easily obtainable through bartering with the indigenous Khoi, as had been done in the past. However, they were to be bitterly disappointed.

Although wildlife was plentiful, the guns of the new arrivals were unsuitable for shooting small game and the settlers were initially unskilled in setting traps. Their guns were also ineffective for shooting big game, as illustrated by Van Riebeeck's journal entry on 24 April 1652 where he describes the unsuccessful shots fired at a hippopotamus. Even hundreds of shots fired at a rhinoceros in 1655, while the animal was trapped in a saltpan, couldn't kill it. Finally, the hungry and desperate hunters cut a hole in the rib cage of the rhinoceros, through which it was shot dead! Attempts to kill whales and hippopotami with canons were also unsuccessful because the animals moved outside striking distance.

Another problem influencing the supply of meat was the decimation of livestock and poultry by wild animals, despite herders sleeping in the pens. In one such instance in August 1653, all the geese and ducks bought from passing ships the previous month were devoured by wild animals. Available livestock was supplied to the ships and the Company's workers had to be content with meat from seals, dassies (rock hyraxes) and sea birds, especially penguins and cormorants.

It was only in 1659 that the Dutch East India Company's herds of sheep and cattle and pigs, rabbits, doves, chickens, ducks, geese and turkeys, were sufficient to supply the local demand for livestock. Wild birds, such as sparrows, weavers, partridges, pelicans, bustards and even flamingos, also became sought after as a source of meat and their popularity as a favourite food was still evident at the beginning of the twentieth century at the Cape market in Darling Street.

The local meat shortage also forced people to use every edible part of the animal, even the soft fat was used for cooking and baking or to spread onto bread instead of butter. The suet was used to make soap or candles.

Cape chicken pie

This is an old Cape recipe for chicken pie made with ham, hard-boiled eggs and salted preserved lemons. Before the first lemon trees planted by Jan van Riebeeck at the Cape could bear fruit, cooks had to rely on salted preserved lemons for their dishes. When lemons became more widely available, the use of salted lemons fell out of favour.

SERVES: 8

CHICKEN
ingredients

1 whole chicken

5 whole cloves

1 Tbsp (15 ml) coriander seeds

2 bay leaves

5 sprigs fresh thyme

12 cups (3 litres) water

300 g salted ham

1 onion

1 carrot

4 cloves garlic

method

Place the chicken and all the spices in a large saucepan and add the water. Bring to the boil, reduce the heat and simmer for 5 minutes, skimming the surface.

Add the rest of the ingredients and simmer for 1 hour until the chicken is tender.

Remove the chicken from the broth and leave to cool. Pick the chicken off the bones and break into small pieces. Discard the skin and bones.

Remove the ham and cut into small cubes.

Strain the broth through a sieve and reserve for chicken stock.

continued ...

continued ...

PIE
ingredients

¼ cup (60 ml) butter

1 onion, chopped

2 cloves garlic

¼ tsp (1 ml) ground cloves

¼ tsp (1 ml) ground coriander

salt and freshly ground black pepper

½ cup (125 ml) cake flour

½ cup (125 ml) preserved lemon rind, chopped (see recipe on page 240)

3 Tbsp (45 ml) chopped fresh parsley

5 hard-boiled eggs, sliced

400 g flaky pastry (see basic recipe on page 253) or 400 g ready-made flaky pastry

1 egg, lightly beaten

method

Preheat the oven to 200 °C (400 °F).

Heat a saucepan and brown 2 Tbsp (30 ml) butter. Add the onion, garlic, cooked and cubed ham and spices and sauté for 5 minutes.

Add the remaining butter as well as the flour. Cook over a low heat for 5 minutes.

Whisk in 4 cups (1 litre) reserved chicken stock and add the lemon, parsley and chicken pieces. Add more stock if the sauce is too thick.

Check seasoning and pour the mixture into an ovenproof dish (20 x 20 cm, x 10 cm deep). Layer the egg slices on top and leave to cool. (Only refrigerate once the chicken is completely cool, to prevent contamination.)

Roll out the pastry on a lightly floured surface and place over the chicken pie mixture, making sure the pastry covers the top of the pie and touches the sides of the dish.

Brush the pastry with beaten egg and make a small incision in the centre of the pastry to allow steam to escape. Bake for 20–30 minutes, until the pastry is golden brown.

Chicken

with green sauce

This recipe was inspired by Thomas van der Noot's recipe (1510) for chicken with 'green sauce'. A similar recipe also appears in another Dutch cookbook from the same century, titled *Wel ende edelike spijse*. The basis of Van der Noot's sauce is chicken stock flavoured with ground ginger, cloves and 'grains of paradise', which is an African spice. In very old recipes, however, cardamom was also often referred to as 'grains of paradise'.

In this recipe the 'grains of paradise' are replaced with peppercorns and cardamom, and instead of thickening the sauce with breadcrumbs and hard-boiled egg yolks as in the original recipe, we use verjuice and egg yolks instead.

SERVES: 4

ingredients

2 Tbsp (30 ml) butter

4 baby chickens

2 onions, chopped

1 clove garlic, sliced

½ cup (125 ml) shelled peas

1 Tbsp (15 ml) chopped fresh root ginger

3 whole cloves

1 tsp (5 ml) cracked black peppercorns

4 cardamom pods

½ cup (125 ml) dry white wine

8 cups (2 litres) chicken stock (see recipe on page 243)

2 cups (2 x 250 ml) picked parsley

3 egg yolks

2 Tbsp (30 ml) verjuice or apple vinegar

salt and freshly ground black pepper

1 Tbsp (15 ml) chopped fresh parsley, for garnishing

method

Heat a stovetop casserole dish or large saucepan and brown the butter. Add the chicken and season with salt. Brown on all sides.

Add the onions, garlic, peas, ginger, cloves, peppercorns and cardamom and sauté for 5 minutes.

Add the white wine and stock, cover with the lid and simmer for 1 hour until the chicken is tender.

Bring a saucepan of water to the boil and add the parsley. Boil for 3 minutes until the parsley is just soft, and then strain and reserve ¼ cup (60 ml) water. Place the reserved water and parsley in a liquidiser and blend until smooth.

Beat together the egg yolks and verjuice, and add the parsley purée. Add this mixture to the dish, reduce the heat and cook until thick and velvety. Season to taste with salt and pepper.

Top with the parsley garnish and serve with basmati rice.

Chicken

with sorrel and lemon

This recipe comes from the cookbook titled *De Verstandige Kock* (ca. 1668). It has basically remained unchanged, which makes this recipe more than 300 years old.

If you are an experienced cook, you can try to preserve lemons yourself. It is more economical than buying them. The best time to do it is during winter, when lemons are plentiful and less expensive. Refer to the recipe on page 240.

Usually only the peel of the lemon is cut up and used in dishes, while the flesh is discarded. The oil from the preserved lemons is fantastic as a glaze over barbecued dishes and can even be used as salad dressing.

SERVES: 4

ingredients

1 whole chicken, deboned and cut into 8 portions

salt and 1 tsp (5 ml) freshly ground black pepper

2 Tbsp (30 ml) butter

1 cup (250 ml) chopped spicy sausage (chorizo, lamb saucisson sec, pork bangers or beef sausage)

1 onion, chopped

1 tsp (5 ml) fresh picked thyme leaves

1 piece mace or ½ tsp (2.5 ml) grated nutmeg

3 cups (750 ml) verjuice

1 preserved lemon, flesh scooped out, peel finely chopped

2 cups (500 ml) sorrel, chopped

1 cup (250 ml) asparagus chunks (optional)

6 egg yolks, beaten (optional)

juice of 1 lemon

method

Season the chicken with salt and black pepper. Heat a stovetop casserole dish or large saucepan and brown the butter. Add the chicken and sausage and brown well on all sides. Add the onion, thyme and mace or nutmeg, and sauté for 5 minutes.

Add the verjuice and preserved lemon, cover and simmer for about 40 minutes until cooked.

Add the sorrel and asparagus and cook for 3 minutes. The sauce should be thick. (If you want to enrich the sauce or thicken it even more, whisk in the egg yolks.) Finish with a pinch of salt and lemon juice.

Serve with freshly baked bread and a rocket or watercress salad.

poultry, meat, game and offal

Chicken
with raisin sauce

This dish was adapted from a sixteenth-century Dutch recipe. Perfect for a quick mid-week meal, the pan-fried and oven-roasted free-range chicken breasts can be prepared at the same time as the sauce. The raisin sauce is also a delight with fish, ham and tongue dishes.

SERVES: 4

CHICKEN
ingredients

4 chicken quarters

4 sprigs fresh thyme

salt and freshly ground black pepper

3 Tbsp (45 ml) soft butter

2 Tbsp (30 ml) olive oil

chopped fresh parsley, for garnishing

method

Preheat the oven to 180 °C (350 °F).

Carefully lift the skin of the thigh and place a sprig of thyme beneath it. Season the skin with salt and pepper and spread the butter on the skin.

Heat a frying pan and add the olive oil. Add the chicken, butter and skin side down, and fry over medium heat until the skin is crispy. Turn the chicken over, place in the oven and roast for 30 minutes.

RAISIN SAUCE
ingredients

2 tsp (10 ml) butter

1 onion, chopped

1 clove garlic, chopped

1 tsp (5 ml) chopped fresh root ginger

pinch of ground cinnamon

1 tsp (5 ml) chopped fresh marjoram

2 Tbsp (30 ml) chopped dried apricots

½ cup (125 ml) raisins or sultanas

3 Tbsp (45 ml) brown sugar

¾ cup (190 ml) white wine vinegar

½ cup (125 ml) sweet wine (muscadel)

½ cup (125 ml) freshly squeezed orange juice

2 Tbsp (30 ml) freshly squeezed lemon juice

1 tsp (5 ml) cold butter

salt and freshly ground black pepper

method

Heat the butter in a saucepan. Sauté the onion, garlic, ginger, cinnamon and marjoram for 5 minutes.

Add the remaining ingredients, except the butter, and cook until the sauce starts to thicken. Beat in the cold butter and season with salt and black pepper to taste.

Place the chicken onto plates and drizzle the sauce over. Sprinkle with chopped parsley and serve with roast or mashed potatoes, roast vegetables or salad.

poultry, meat, game and offal

Meat

baked in a crust

In days of old when refrigerators and freezers didn't exist, one of the methods for preserving cooked meat and preventing it from rotting was to bake it in a hard crust. A firm dough made from rye flour, wheat flour, sorghum flour or maize flour mixed with water and a little oil was prepared to form the crust. It was important not to use too much fat or oil in the dough because the idea was for the crust to be rock-hard. In this way, germs and bacteria couldn't penetrate the crust and contaminate the meat. The dough-encrusted meat was then placed in a pot with coals on top of the lid and underneath the pot, or put in a hole and covered with coals. The baking time could vary up to a few hours, depending on the size of the meat inside the crust.

The oldest recipe found was for a crust made from rye flour as prepared by the Roman chef Apicius. In another recipe from the cookbook *De Verstandige Kock*, wholemeal was used and the meat was cut up into small pieces. Mary Sanderson's cookbook also contains a recipe that follows this same method. Even by the middle of the twentieth century, Mrs Joan Staples from the Karoo was still serving cooked meat baked in a maize flour crust.

Valentyn, a pastor, tells of how he received game in *een steene korst* (one hard crust or, literally, rock crust), while he was on his way from the Cape to the East in 1705. He mentioned that the meat was very enjoyable and that they savoured it for a whole month during their journey. The hard crust around the meat was discarded when the contents had to be used. This method doesn't just preserve the meat for a long period, it also traps moisture inside the meat to keep it deliciously tender.

Chestnut trees were in abundance at the Cape during the time of the first settlers. The chestnut stuffing in this recipe can be replaced with any other kind of stuffing. Cubed meat or game, or whole deboned meat joints such as leg of lamb can be successfully prepared and preserved with this method.

SERVES: 6

MEAT

ingredients

1 duck, giblets removed

¼ cup (60 ml) coarse sea salt

½ cup (125 ml) red wine

1 Tbsp (15 ml) brown sugar

1 tsp (5 ml) chopped fresh root ginger

2 cups (500 ml) water chestnuts, peeled and boiled
or 1 x 450 g can whole chestnuts, drained

1 cup (250 ml) fresh breadcrumbs

1 Tbsp (15 ml) melted butter

½ cup (125 ml) currants

½ tsp (2.5 ml) ground cinnamon

½ tsp (2.5 ml) grated nutmeg

pinch of ground cloves

1 Tbsp (15 ml) chopped dried orange peel

method

Score the duck skin by piercing it all over with a
fork. Make sure to season the abdominal cavity.

Rub the salt into the skin and refrigerate overnight.
The next day, rinse the salt off and pat dry.

Place the wine, sugar and ginger in a saucepan
over high heat and stir to dissolve the sugar. Bring
to the boil for 5 minutes.

Place the remaining ingredients in a blender and
process into a paste. Add the wine mixture and
place in the refrigerator for 1 hour.

Push the stuffing loosely into the abdominal cavity
and truss the bird by tying the legs and wings
together with string close to the duck's body. Set
aside while you make the crust.

CRUST

ingredients

½ cup (125 ml) lamb fat or lard

3 cups (750 ml) cake flour

warm water

method

Rub the fat into the flour and add just enough
water to make a coarse paste.

Cover the whole duck with the paste to about
3 mm thick and set aside in the refrigerator to dry,
preferably overnight.

The following day, place the duck in hot coals –
place some coals on top too – and leave to cook
for 2–3 hours.

Break open the crust, remove the duck, cut off the
string and carve the bird.

Serve with a sweet-and-sour cherry sauce (see
Duck in Sweet-and-sour Sauce, page 103).

 Duck

in sweet-and-sour sauce

The Romans were the first to use must in their cooking. Instead of adding wine to food and letting it evaporate, they prepared three types of *moskonfyt* (must jam) with various consistencies for use in different dishes.

The origins of this recipe can be traced back to the Italian chef Scappi (1570). A similar recipe also appears in an eighteenth-century Cape cookbook.

SERVES: 4

ingredients

1 duck

1 cup (250 ml) coarse sea salt

1 onion, chopped

1 cup (250 ml) must syrup (available from wine farms and farm stalls)

½ cup (125 ml) red wine vinegar

¼ cup (60 ml) verjuice

½ cup (125 ml) Cape gooseberries or dried cherries

2 unripe plums, chopped

1 cinnamon stick, 1 tsp (5 ml) black peppercorns and 2 whole cloves, wrapped in a muslin bag

2 cloves garlic, crushed

1 Tbsp (15 ml) chopped fresh root ginger

1 tsp (5 ml) cold butter

method

Prick the skin of the duck with a fork and cover with the salt. Refrigerate overnight. Wipe off the salt with a clean, wet cloth.

Preheat the oven to 120 °C (250 °F).

Grease the oven rack and place the salted duck on the rack.

Scatter the chopped onion in a drip tray and place it underneath the duck.

Roast the duck for 6 hours. Turn the heat up to 160 °C (325 °F) and roast for a further 20 minutes. Remove from the oven and set aside.

Place the onions from the drip tray, the must syrup, vinegar, verjuice, gooseberries or dried cherries, plums, spice bag, garlic and ginger in a saucepan and cook until thick. Discard the spice bag and beat in the cold butter.

Carve the duck and serve with the sauce.

Cape frikkadelle

Frikkadelle (meatballs) were prepared by the Persians and Romans many centuries ago. It was a popular dish at the Cape and was most often stewed or braised, but sometimes fried in shallow fat. There were many variations of the recipe.

The old Persian recipe in which raw meat was wrapped around shelled hard-boiled eggs, before it was fried in shallow fat, was well-known at the Cape. Before serving, these *frikkadelle* were halved and then dished with fried sweet-and-sour onions.

The Greek variation of meatballs wrapped in cabbage or vine leaves also became popular amongst the old Persians. The Dutch used lettuce leaves to wrap the *frikkadelle*.

Meatballs made of peacock meat were extremely popular at the Cape. The Romans loved them too and Roman cook Apicius recorded a peacock *frikkadel* recipe.

MAKES: 35 frikkadelle

ingredients

1 head firm cos lettuce, or lettuce of your choice, or cabbage

¼ cup (60 ml) butter

1 onion, chopped

2 cloves garlic, chopped

1 tsp (5 ml) chopped fresh root ginger

¼ tsp (1 ml) grated nutmeg, or more to taste

¼ tsp (1 ml) ground cloves, or more to taste

1 tsp (5 ml) salt

¼ tsp (1 ml) ground white pepper, or more to taste

½ cup (125 ml) apple cider vinegar

½ cup (125 ml) brown sugar

¼ cup (60 ml) fruit chutney

2 kg lamb or beef, minced

500 g pork, minced

2 Tbsp (30 ml) chopped fresh coriander or parsley (optional)

¾ cup (190 ml) water or meat stock (see recipes on pages 242–243)

method

Preheat the oven to 180 °C (350 °F).

Loosen all the lettuce or cabbage leaves from the stem and remove the thick vein from each leaf with a sharp knife. Place the leaves in a large saucepan with boiling water and simmer for 30 seconds.

Remove the leaves with a slotted spoon and refresh immediately in iced water. Leave to cool for a few minutes, and then remove the lettuce or cabbage from the water, dry and set aside in the refrigerator.

Heat 2 Tbsp (30 ml) of the butter in a large saucepan and add the onion, garlic, ginger, spices and seasoning, and sauté until the onion is tender.

Add the vinegar, sugar and chutney and cook until the mixture is thick and syrupy. Remove from the heat and leave to cool to room temperature.

Place the mince, chutney pickle and coriander or parsley (if using) in a large bowl and mix well. Season with salt to taste.

Roll the mince into 80 g balls and cut the lettuce leaves into 10 x 5 cm strips. Wrap each frikkadel in a lettuce or cabbage leaf and secure with a toothpick.

Place the frikkadelle in a greased ovenproof dish and dot with the remaining butter. Add a little water or stock and cover the dish with a lid or foil. Bake in the oven for 25 minutes.

The frikkadelle can be served immediately or can be reheated. They can also be enjoyed cold on a long road trip.

Sweet-and-sour
pumpkin and lamb stew

Before Christopher Columbus 'discovered' the Americas in 1494, cooks following the Persian-Arabian culinary tradition had to rely on a type of calabash pumpkin that couldn't be used when ripe (the pumpkin dried out and became hollow as it ripened). Therefore they prepared green pumpkin stew.

 Jan van Riebeeck planted South American pumpkins at the Cape quite early on and these large white pumpkins became so popular that they were later known as *boerpampoen*. They were served as vegetables during the winter and were suitable as rations on the many ships that docked in Table Bay. At the Cape, green pumpkins were used in early summer for stews, while ripe pumpkins were used in winter.

SERVES: 6–8

MARINADE
ingredients

1 onion, chopped

4 cloves garlic, chopped

1 cup (250 ml) good-quality red wine

½ cup (125 ml) dry sherry

½ cup (125 ml) wine vinegar

3 Tbsp (45 ml) pumpkin seeds

1 tsp (5 ml) salt

1 tsp (5 ml) freshly ground black pepper

½ tsp (2.5 ml) ground ginger

½ tsp (2.5 ml) ground cinnamon

pinch of saffron

2 Tbsp (30 ml) chopped fresh mint

½ cup (125 ml) whole almonds, blanched

1 tsp (5 ml) fennel seeds, crushed

2 Tbsp (30 ml) honey

method

Place all the marinade ingredients in an earthenware dish and marinate the lamb in this mixture for 3–4 hours.

PUMPKIN AND LAMB
ingredients

1.2 kg lamb breast, cut into chunks

2 Tbsp (30 ml) olive oil

4 cups (1 litre) lamb stock (see recipe on page 243) or water

2 cups (500 ml) fresh greenish apricots, cut into chunks, or ½ cup (125 ml) dried apricots

1 cup (250 ml) buttermilk

2 cups (500 ml) diced pumpkin (if using green pumpkin, remember to reduce the liquid as the pumpkin draws a lot of water)

salt and freshly ground black pepper

method

Preheat the oven to 160 °C (325 °F).

Remove the meat from the marinade and pat dry. Discard the marinade.

Heat the olive oil in a large frying pan and brown the meat in the hot oil.

Place the meat, stock, apricots and buttermilk in an oven casserole with a tight-fitting lid and bake in the oven for 3 hours, or until almost tender. Add the pumpkin and cook, uncovered, for about 20 minutes until done.

Season to taste with salt and pepper. Serve with crusty bread or rice and a sambal.

Veal carbonade

Carbonade is the French term for meat quickly grilled in a pan or over the coals and served medium-rare.

In 1710, the granddaughter of Jan van Riebeeck mentioned the Cape *karmoenade* she enjoyed and, in 1797, Johanna Duminy wrote about the *carmonaade* prepared for lunch from two legs of lamb, on their arrival at the farm where they hunted game. Lady Anne Barnard, who lived at the Cape between 1797 and 1798, also describes in her letter to Henry Dundas a delightful breakfast where crumbed *carbonade* seasoned with parsley was served.

Apart from parsley, seasoning such as lemon zest and juice, thyme and marjoram were also used in preparing the *carbonade*. In the Cape recipe recorded by Hewitt in 1890, the meat was marinated for an hour in a mixture of ground ginger, chopped onions and parsley before it was crumbed and baked.

In this version of the dish, veal chops are used. The chops are served with a parsley butter sauce with a surprising twist – the butter is frozen, crumbed and fried in oil. When the butter is served, it consists of a small, melting ball wrapped in a crusty layer of crumbs.

SERVES: 4

VEAL
ingredients

1½ cups (375 ml) dried breadcrumbs

1 Tbsp (15 ml) chopped fresh parsley

½ tsp (2.5 ml) salt

½ tsp (2.5 ml) freshly ground black pepper

4 veal chops, French trimmed (rib bone cleaned)

cake flour, for dusting

2 egg whites, lightly beaten

2 Tbsp (30 ml) butter

method

Preheat the oven to 180 °C (350 °F).

Mix the crumbs, parsley, salt and pepper.

Lightly dust the veal chops in flour, coat in egg white and toss in the crumb mixture.

Repeat the egg white and crumb process so that you end up with double-crumbed chops.

Place in the oven for 5 minutes, for medium-rare. Transfer the chops to a heated frying pan and brown the chops in butter on both sides.

PARSLEY BUTTER SAUCE
ingredients

200 g butter, room temperature

2 Tbsp (30 ml) finely minced fresh parsley

½ tsp (2.5 ml) finely minced garlic

½ tsp (2.5 ml) lemon zest

½ tsp (2.5 ml) salt

¼ tsp (1 ml) freshly ground black pepper

2 egg whites, lightly beaten

1 cup (250 ml) dried breadcrumbs or rusk crumbs

method

Place all the ingredients, except the egg and crumbs, in a bowl and beat for 3–5 minutes to mix. Pour into a dish and refrigerate.

Use a melon baller or Parisian scoop to make small butter balls.

Place the balls in the freezer until rock hard. Crumb using the same process as for the chops.

Fry in hot oil just until the crumbs turn golden brown and serve immediately, spooned on top of the chops.

Serve with quince preserve and a healthy salad.

NOTE:

A batter can also be used for the meat instead of the crumbs.

Roast saddle of lamb

Within a few years of Jan van Riebeeck's arrival at the Cape, there were enough sheep to supply the population with all the mutton they needed. O.F. Mentzel, a German soldier who came to the Cape in 1733, mentions that most farmers kept fat-tailed sheep. According to him, preference was given to hoggets (yearlings). These terms refer to fully grown sheep less than two years old.

In contrast with the buying patterns of consumers today, who mainly prefer lamb, the meat of young, fully grown sheep is of better quality in many respects. The meat of these sheep is more flavoursome and the fat ratio is usually lower than that of lamb, as well as it being a more economical choice.

Saddle of mutton was a popular cut of meat at the Cape. Leftover saddle of mutton was also served cold for breakfast, processed for use in pies or *bobotie*, or was stewed for fricassée.

SERVES: 6

ingredients

5 cloves garlic

2 Tbsp (30 ml) chopped fresh rosemary

1 Tbsp (15 ml) chopped fresh marjoram

1 Tbsp (15 ml) lemon zest

4 Tbsp (60 ml) olive oil

2 tsp (10 ml) coriander seeds, crushed

2 tsp (10 ml) freshly ground black pepper

2 tsp (10 ml) coarse sea salt

½ tsp (2.5 ml) grated nutmeg

1 tsp (5 ml) ground cumin

1 saddle of lamb, deboned (loin, fillet and belly flap intact)

2 cups (500 ml) dried apricots

1 Tbsp (15 ml) butter

method

Preheat the oven to 120 °C (250 °F).

Place the garlic, rosemary, marjoram, lemon zest and 2 Tbsp (30 ml) olive oil in a mortar and grind to a paste.

Add the coriander seeds, pepper, salt, nutmeg and cumin, and then rub the mixture into the meat. Place the apricots down the centre of the saddle and roll up the meat tightly. Secure with string.

Heat a large frying pan and add the remaining olive oil and the butter. Brown the meat on all sides and place on a roasting tray. Roast in the oven for 6 hours.

Remove from the oven and leave to rest for 30 minutes. Heat a little more oil in a frying pan and slowly crisp up the outer fat layer, or place the meat under a preheated grill for a few minutes.

Carve and serve.

Salted lamb's rib
(Soutribbetjie)

Curing meat was a way of preserving it during the long summer months. If the meat couldn't be used shortly after butchering, it was hung up to dry out completely. Thereafter it was placed in water to swell before it was cooked until tender and then grilled over the coals.

SERVES: 6

ingredients

1 lamb's rib, deboned

¼ cup (60 ml) coarse sea salt

2 Tbsp (30 ml) brown sugar

1 Tbsp (15 ml) freshly ground black pepper

½ tsp (2.5 ml) ground cardamom

1 tsp (5 ml) grated nutmeg

1 Tbsp (15 ml) cracked coriander seeds

pinch of ground cloves

2 sprigs fresh rosemary

2 sprigs fresh thyme, picked

method

Score the fatty outside layer of the meat with a sharp knife, making shallow incisions all over.

Mix the salt, sugar and all the spices and herbs together and rub the mixture well into the meat. Roll up tightly and tie with butcher's string. Place in the refrigerator or a cool place for 48 hours.

Cold-smoke the rib or hang it in a chimney for two days.

To prepare the meat for cooking, place it in a saucepan, cover with cold water, add some herbs of choice and simmer for 1½–2 hours until the meat is tender.

Remove the meat from the water, cut off the string and flatten it out. Refrigerate until ready to grill.

Grill over a hot fire until the fat is crispy.

Serve with corn on the cob grilled over the coals and Cape Mixed Salad (see recipe on page 169).

Boer goat terrine

Even before the arrival of Jan van Riebeeck at the Cape, the indigenous people kept goats as part of their herds of livestock. In 1661, an expedition travelling from the Cape came upon a tribe of Namaquas who kept these goats in the Clanwilliam region.

The origins of these goats are not clear, but they probably found their way to the Cape from North Africa. Through breeding with imported Swiss milk goats, the indigenous goats were refined to the boer goat species we know today.

The meat of boer goats was very popular in the past, as it is exceptionally tender and succulent because of the equal distribution of fat in the meat. Goat's meat contains a high percentage of protein and iron. The cholesterol and unsaturated fat content is the lowest among the twelve types of meat generally eaten in South Africa.

This recipe using goat's meat is very complex and not for the inexperienced cook, as it requires some expert culinary knowledge and skills.

SERVES: 10

PART 1: CONFIT OF SHOULDER AND BACON

ingredients

2 Tbsp (30 ml) coarse sea salt

2 tsp (10 ml) brown sugar

1 tsp (5 ml) ground coriander

1 boer goat shoulder, deboned

4 cups (4 x 250 ml) duck fat or butter

200 g smoked bacon, in one piece

2 cloves garlic

2 sprigs fresh rosemary

salt and freshly ground black pepper

method

Rub the salt, sugar and coriander into the shoulder and refrigerate overnight.

Heat 1 cup (250 ml) of duck fat or butter, add the bacon and brown on all sides.

Add the remaining duck fat or butter, garlic, rosemary and the shoulder.

Place parchment (baking) paper or greaseproof paper on the surface and simmer. It should make slow bubbles, but not boil rapidly. Cook for 4 hours until very soft and skim off the fat. (The shoulder can also be preserved in the fat for up to 6 months.)

Discard the rosemary and garlic and cut the bacon and shoulder into 1 cm chunks. Season with salt and black pepper. Set aside.

continued …

continued …

Part 2: Braised neck and wine jelly

ingredients

3 Tbsp (45 ml) olive oil

½ tsp (2.5 ml) coarse sea salt

½ tsp (2.5 ml) freshly ground black pepper

1 tsp (5 ml) finely chopped fresh rosemary

1 tsp (5 ml) lemon zest

2 boer goat necks

1 Tbsp (15 ml) butter

8 pickling onions, peeled

1 carrot, cut into 4 pieces

2 stalks celery, cut into chunks

1 tsp (5 ml) coriander seeds

¼ cup (60 ml) dried mushrooms

4 cloves garlic, minced

2 whole cloves

2 cups (500 ml) good-quality red wine

1 cup (250 ml) port

12 cups (3 litres) veal stock (see recipe on page 243)

12 leaves gelatin or 4 Tbsp (60 ml) powdered gelatin

method

Preheat the oven to 180 °C (350 °F).

Mix 1 Tbsp (15 ml) olive oil with the salt, pepper, rosemary and lemon zest. Rub this mixture into the necks and marinate overnight.

Heat a casserole dish that can be used on the stovetop and is large enough to hold both necks. Add the butter and remaining olive oil and brown the butter.

Add the necks and brown well on all sides. Remove from the pan and set aside.

Add the onions, carrot, celery, coriander seeds, dried mushrooms, garlic and cloves to the casserole and sauté for 5 minutes.

Pour in the wine and port and reduce to a syrupy consistency. Skim off the fat.

Add the necks and stock. Fit the lid and place in the oven for 4 hours until soft. Remove the meat from the cooking liquid and pick all the meat off the bones. Set aside.

Strain the cooking liquid. Skim all the fat off the top and pour the liquid into a measuring jug. You'll need about 6 cups (1.5 litres) of cooking liquid for the jelly.

To make the jelly, soften the gelatin in ice water. Heat just over ¾ cup (200 ml) of the cooking liquid, add the softened gelatin and stir until dissolved. Add the remaining cooking liquid to the hot jelly and stir to mix. Don't add the hot to the cold liquid, as it will set into a ball and not diffuse properly.

Place the jelly in the refrigerator and leave to set. It should be firm to the touch, but not like rubber.

Part 3: Braised neck mixture

ingredients

1 onion, finely chopped

2 gherkins, finely chopped

1 Tbsp (15 ml) capers, chopped

½ tsp (2.5 ml) truffle oil

1 porcini mushroom, chopped and sautéed

picked meat from the necks

2 Tbsp (30 ml) snipped chives

salt and freshly ground black pepper

method

Mix the onion, gherkins, capers, truffle oil, porcini, meat and chives. Season with salt and pepper and refrigerate until needed.

Part 4: Cured goat fillets

ingredients

300 g brown sugar

100 g coarse sea salt

1 Tbsp (15 ml) dried buchu powder (or use buchu tea, available from health shops or pharmacies)

2 tsp (10 ml) coriander seeds

2 tsp (10 ml) black peppercorns

4 boer goat fillets

1 Tbsp (15 ml) vegetable oil

method

Mix the sugar, salt, buchu, coriander seeds and peppercorns together.

Place the fillets on a large sheet of foil.

Rub the dry mixture into the meat and roll into a sausage shape with the foil. Fold over the ends and refrigerate for 12 hours.

Remove the meat from the foil, rinse off and pat dry with paper towel. Heat a large frying pan. Add the oil and brown the fillets well, but no longer than 3 minutes. Leave to cool.

Assembly of terrine

ingredients

20–30 slices of ham or prosciutto

braised neck mixture

cured boer goat fillets

8–12 cooked artichoke hearts

confit of shoulder and bacon

wine jelly

method

Line a terrine mould or rectangular dish (20 cm long x 5 cm wide x 5 cm deep) with plastic wrap (first rub the mould with soft butter so that the plastic will cling to the sides of the mould), making sure to press the plastic well into the corners. Make sure that the plastic wrap extends over the sides of the mould so that they will overlap when folded over the the terrine.

Line the mould with the slices of ham, making sure they overlap each other and extend far enough over the sides of the mould so that they will meet each other again if you fold them towards the middle.

Press three-quarters of the braised neck mixture into the mould.

Place the whole fillets on top in two rows, followed by the artichokes, also in two rows.

Press the remaining braised neck mixture into all the gaps.

Layer the chunky confit of shoulder and bacon, not higher than 4 mm from the top. Press down to get an even layer.

Melt the jelly, making sure not to let it get too hot. If the gelatin is boiled, it loses its setting properties.

Pour the jelly slowly into the mould, and at 2-minute intervals, so it runs into all the gaps. Do not rush this step, otherwise you will have air bubbles in the end product.

Fold the overlapping ham onto the surface, followed by the plastic wrap. Your terrine should stick out 2–3 mm above the rim of the mould. Place the mould on a tray.

Place another tray or mould on top and weigh it down in the refrigerator for at least 12 hours. Some jelly will run out, so make sure the tray at the bottom has a lip.

To turn out the terrine, carefully turn the mould upside down on a board and pull one end of the plastic onto the board. Carefully unmould.

Slice the terrine with a sharp carving knife and serve with toasted sourdough bread, apricot and peach chutney and a honey-roasted swede purée.

Game neck potjie

The original way of cooking at the Cape in the seventeenth and eighteenth centuries is what is today called 'slow food'. The development of the Slow Food Movement is a rebellion against modern fast food and promotes, among other things, respect for nature, food, the farmer who produces the food, and the protection of cultural traditions.

SERVES: 8

ingredients

2 onions, sliced

2 Tbsp (30 ml) olive oil

300 g belly bacon or smoked kassler chops, diced

2 kg deboned kudu neck, cut into chunks (bones reserved for stock), or use any other kind of venison

cake flour, for dusting

1 tsp (5 ml) ground cinnamon

pinch of ground cloves

¼ cup (60 ml) chopped fresh parsley

1 Tbsp (15 ml) brown sugar

zest and juice of 1 lemon

½ cup (125 ml) quince jelly or grape jam

3 cups (750 ml) good-quality dry red wine

16 baby carrots

1 pkt (250 g) dried pears

venison stock (see recipe on page 244)

1 cup (250 ml) buttermilk

1 tsp (5 ml) freshly ground black pepper

method

Heat a cast-iron three-legged pot over open flames. Sauté the onions in oil and add the bacon. Sauté for another 3 minutes and remove from the pot. Set aside.

Dust the neck lightly with flour and brown in the pot. Add the cinnamon, cloves, parsley, sugar and lemon zest and cook for 5 minutes.

Return the onions and bacon to the pot. Add the lemon juice, quince jelly or grape jam, and red wine and reduce by three-quarters.

Add the carrots and pears and just enough stock to cover everything.

Cover with the lid and do not open for 3–4 hours. Adjust the coals under the pot from time to time in order for the pot to keep simmering.

Remove the lid and add the buttermilk once the sauce has thickened. Do not overstir. Check seasoning and serve with rice or *mieliepap* (maize porridge).

Game pie

The traditional method for making game pie by stewing the game with marrowbones and/or strips of unsmoked pork/bacon (*spek*) or mutton tail fat and a combination of spices – such as cloves, ginger, cinnamon, allspice, coriander, pepper, nutmeg, and bay leaves, and brown sugar, vinegar and wine – is still in use today in the Cape Winelands. In the original recipe bacon could be substituted with marrow for added richness. Some cooks prefer to add herbs such as thyme, sage and rosemary.

SERVES: 8

ingredients

1 kg venison shoulder or leg, cubed

200 g smoked bacon, cut into thin strips

3 cups (750 ml) good-quality dry red wine

1 tsp (5 ml) ground cinnamon

6 whole cloves (wrapped in a muslin bag)

¼ tsp (1 ml) ground ginger

pinch of saffron (optional)

2 Tbsp (30 ml) lamb's tail fat, lard or oil

salt and freshly ground black pepper

1 onion, chopped

1 cup (250 ml) dried peaches

2 Tbsp (30 ml) tamarind, dissolved in 1 cup (250 ml) water or ¼ cup (60 ml) vinegar

2 Tbsp (30 ml) brown sugar

8 cups (2 litres) venison, beef or lamb stock (see recipes on pages 243–244) or water

1 buttermilk pastry (see recipe on page 253)

milk, for brushing

freshly ground sea salt

method

Place the venison, bacon, wine, cinnamon, cloves, ginger and saffron (if using) in an earthenware dish and marinate overnight.

The following day, preheat the oven to 160 °C (325 °F).

Use a large, heavy-based casserole dish with a tight-fitting lid that can also be used on the stovetop, heat it and add the fat, lard or oil.

Remove the venison and bacon from the marinade (reserve the marinade) and pat dry with paper towel. Season with the salt and pepper and brown in the fat.

Add the onion and fry for 5 minutes.

Add the peaches, tamarind water or vinegar, sugar, reserved marinade and stock. Fit the lid and place in the oven for 2–3 hours until soft.

Place the dish on the stove and cook until the sauce thickens or add a little cornflour mixed with water.

Check seasoning and leave to cool in the pot.

Increase the oven temperature to 200 °C (400 °F).

Place the pastry on a lightly floured surface and roll out 2 cm thick to the size of the casserole pot. Place on top of the meat, covering the whole surface. Alternatively, you can make little balls of pastry and place them tightly next to each other on top of the meat.

Brush the surface with milk and sprinkle with freshly ground sea salt. Bake for about 45 minutes until golden brown.

Wildebeest sirloin

with cameline sauce

A spiced sauce thickened with bread was so popular during the Middle Ages that it could be purchased ready-made from hawkers peddling their wares in fourteenth-century Paris. This spiced sauce was known as *cameline sous*. In *Le Ménagier de Paris* (ca. 1393) the husband advises his young bride to buy cameline and sorrel sauce at the market for his dinner.

The Dutch would have been very familiar with this sauce when they arrived at the Cape and we can assume that it was frequently served as an accompaniment to meat dishes.

Taillevent, master chef to the French king during the fourteenth century, developed a version of cameline sauce that we have adapted here.

SERVES: 2–4

SIRLOIN
ingredients

½ tsp (2.5 ml) salt

500 g wildebeest sirloin, sinew removed

2 cups (500 ml) good-quality dry red wine

1 Tbsp (15 ml) black peppercorns

2 Tbsp (30 ml) chopped fresh root ginger

2 cinnamon sticks

½ tsp (2.5 ml) grated nutmeg

pinch of saffron

2 Tbsp (30 ml) brown sugar

1 cup (250 ml) water

1 Tbsp (15 ml) butter

1 Tbsp (15 ml) sunflower oil

method

Rub the salt into the meat and refrigerate for 1 hour.

Place the remaining ingredients in a saucepan and bring to the boil. Leave to cool.

Once cool, pour the marinade over the meat and refrigerate overnight.

The following day, remove the meat and pat dry. Reserve the marinade.

Preheat the oven to 220 °C (425 °F).

Heat 1 Tbsp (15 ml) olive oil in a frying pan and add 1 tsp (5 ml) butter. Add the meat and brown well.

Place the meat in the oven and cook to desired doneness; 3–4 minutes for medium-rare.

CAMELINE SAUCE
ingredients

reserved marinade

8 cups (2 litres) veal stock (see recipe on page 243)

pinch of saffron

pinch of ground cinnamon

pinch of ground ginger

salt and freshly ground black pepper

2–3 Tbsp (30–45 ml) butter

method

Place the marinade in a saucepan and reduce over high heat to a glaze. Add the stock and spices and reduce the sauce again until thick and syrupy. Season to taste with salt and pepper.

Whisk in the butter to thicken.

Serve with the wildebeest sirloin, honey-roasted parsnips and sautéed broad beans.

Offal sult

Sult (brawn) was a dish traditionally prepared on the day the animal was slaughtered. In Europe, pig's head and trotters were used to make *sult*, while at the Cape, where mutton was mainly on offer, sheep's offal with extra mutton added, constituted the main ingredients.

After the arrival of the French Huguenots in the late seventeenth century, offal was often prepared by cooking sheep's tripe together with the head and trotters, and thus the tripe became part of the *sult*.

SERVES: 12

ingredients

1 pig's head, cleaned

1 pork hock, smoked

4 sheep's trotters

2 Tbsp (30 ml) coarse sea salt

40 cups (10 litres) water

4 carrots, washed and chopped in big chunks

2 onions, peeled and quartered

1 stalk celery, washed and chopped into 4 pieces

¼-piece whole nutmeg

1 Tbsp (15 ml) black peppercorns

1 Tbsp (15 ml) coriander seeds

3 bay leaves

10 whole cloves

4 whole allspice

3 Tbsp (45 ml) white wine vinegar

2 cloves garlic, chopped

1 Tbsp (15 ml) fresh picked thyme

½ tsp (2.5 ml) freshly ground black pepper

salt

6 hard-boiled eggs, grated (optional)

1 Tbsp (15 ml) chopped fresh parsley (optional)

method

Place the cleaned pig's head, hock and trotters with the salt in a very large saucepan and cover with the water. Bring to the boil, reduce the heat and simmer for 1 hour, skimming all the time.

Add the carrots, onions and celery. Place the nutmeg, peppercorns, coriander seeds, bay leaves, cloves and allspice in a muslin bag. Add to the saucepan with the vinegar and simmer for 2–3 hours more until the meat is tender and half the liquid has evaporated.

Cool slightly and remove the head, hock and trotters. Pick all the meat off the bones and cut into small cubes. Set aside.

Strain the cooking liquid. Keep the fat that solidifies on the top as it cools. (If you want to keep this fat refrigerated for a long time, cover with a layer of fat that has been strained through muslin cloth.)

Add the garlic, thyme and pepper to the strained liquid, and simmer until reduced by half. Add salt to taste. Combine the cooked and picked meat and eggs and parsley (if using) in a bowl and season lightly with salt and pepper.

Line a large rectangular mould or loaf pan with plastic wrap and press the meat mixture into the mould. Pour the strained liquid over and refrigerate for a minimum of 12 hours.

Serve with capers, stewed sour apples, *boerejongens* (brandied grapes) and Cape ham.

Rolpens
(andoelie)

The Dutch *rolpens* made at the Cape since 1652 was a stuffed sheep's stomach. The stuffing was made with long strips of meat, fat, spices and some rice or barley. Sometimes raisins were added. The French Huguenots, who came to the Cape in 1688, used the sheep's stomach with the head and trotters as part of their offal dish. They used the large intestine instead of the stomach to make a version of *rolpens*, which they called *andouille*. They preferred pork, fat, offal and offcuts of meat with herbs and spices as a stuffing, but no cereal was used.

The *rolpens* was cooked and pressed and sometimes smoked. To serve it hot, slices of rolpens were crumbed and fried in fat or butter and then served with vinegar, fried bananas or sour apples.

Over time these two different recipes were combined and any meat offcuts, offal and even pluck were used by some cooks for a stuffing.

SERVES: 6

ingredients

2–3 sheep's stomachs, sliced into 12 strips measuring 5 x 10 cm

12 strips (2 cm wide) thinly sliced Cape ham (optional)

12 strips (2 cm wide) thinly sliced pickled ox tongue

12 strips (2 cm wide) thinly sliced smoked pork belly

salt and freshly ground black pepper

8– 12 cups (2–3 litres) strong lamb stock (see recipe on page 243)

¾ cup (190 ml) good-quality dry red wine

2 Tbsp (30 ml) white wine vinegar

1 onion, chopped in large chunks

3 bay leaves

1 sprig fresh sage

6 whole cloves

6 whole allspice

1 tsp (5 ml) grated nutmeg

1 tsp (5 ml) ground coriander

1 tsp (5 ml) ground cumin

method

Preheat the oven to 160 °C (325 °F).

Flatten each stomach strip so the length is facing away from you.

Start 1 cm from the edge of the stomach and layer the ham (if using), tongue and pork belly on top of each other. Season with salt and pepper between the layers.

Fold the stomach over and roll up tightly. Tie up the stomach with string, securing both ends and wrapping the string around it a few times. Repeat with the rest of the strips until you have 12 rolls.

Place the rolls in a heavy-based ovenproof dish. Add the stock, wine, vinegar, onion, bay leaves, sage and spices. Place parchment (baking) paper on the surface and braise in the oven for 3–4 hours, until the rolls are tender and cooked through.

Carefully lift out the rolls, set aside and cool. Strain the liquid and reserve for the sauce.

continued …

continued ...

Curry sauce
ingredients

2 Tbsp (30 ml) sunflower oil

1 onion, chopped

1 clove garlic, chopped

1 carrot, finely diced

1 stalk celery, finely diced

zest and juice of 1 lemon

1 tsp (5 ml) chopped fresh root ginger

3 Tbsp (45 ml) curry mix 3 (see recipe on page 248)

reserved cooking liquid)

1 Tbsp (15 ml) currants

1 Tbsp (15 ml) chopped dried apricots

1 Tbsp (15 ml) chopped dried figs

1 Tbsp (15 ml) butter (optional)

method

Heat the oil in a saucepan and sweat the onion, garlic, carrot, celery, lemon zest and ginger until tender.

Roast the curry spice in a dry frying pan and then add it to the onion mixture in the saucepan.

Add enough cooking liquid from the stomach to cover the onion and spice mixture and the dried fruit and simmer for 10–15 minutes until the sauce starts to thicken.

If using, whisk in the butter until it thickens the sauce.

Remove the string from the stomach rolls, place the rolls in the sauce and gently heat through.

Serve with rice or mashed potatoes, and fruit chutney.

Pickled ox tongue

with anchovy and caper sauce

Fresh, salted, smoked and sweet-and-sour ox tongue were favourite dishes enjoyed at the Cape. The ox tongue was usually stewed in red wine together with a little sugar and spices such as salt, pepper, cloves, nutmeg, ginger and cinnamon. Sometimes sour apples would be added to the stew. Today, sweet-and-sour ox tongue is still savoured by many, but it is cooked in water instead of wine.

  This recipe calls for a sweet-and-sour sauce to be served with the pickled tongue. The piquant capers and salty anchovies are the perfect taste companions for a rich dish such as tongue.

SERVES: 4-6

TONGUE PICKLE
ingredients

1 ox tongue

4 cups (1 litre) water

1 pkt (250 g) coarse sea salt

⅓ cup (80 ml) brown sugar

2 sprigs fresh thyme

2 cloves garlic, sliced

1 Tbsp (15 ml) black peppercorns

1 Tbsp (15 ml) coriander seeds

2 bay leaves

bouquet garni (bay leaf, parsley, thyme, onion, clove and celery)

method

Clean the tongue, remove all the glands and rinse under cold running water.

Put the tongue into a large glass container. Place the rest of the ingredients in a large saucepan and boil for 1 minute. Pour the cooking liquid over the tongue, making sure the tongue is covered. Refrigerate for 24 hours.

Rinse the tongue and place back in the refrigerator until ready to cook. (The tongue can also be cold-smoked.) Alternatively, you can buy pickled or ready-smoked tongue.

Place the tongue in a large saucepan, cover completely with water and add the bouquet garni.

Poach the tongue in the water for 3–4 hours, or until tender. Peel off the skin and let the tongue cool in the cooking liquid. Slice thinly and set aside.

ANCHOVY AND CAPER SAUCE
ingredients

2 anchovy fillets

1 tsp (5 ml) capers

1 Tbsp (15 ml) vinegar

1 cup (250 ml) beef stock (see recipe on page 243)

1 Tbsp (15 ml) brown sugar or honey

method

Mix all the ingredients together in a saucepan and bring to the boil. Add the slices of tongue, reduce the heat and simmer for 10 minutes.

Remove the tongue and arrange on a platter. Increase the heat and cook the sauce further until thick, reduced and syrupy.

Pour the sauce over the slices and leave for at least 1 hour for the flavours to marry. Serve cold.

Pan-fried liver

with sweet-and-sour pomegranate sauce

The use of pomegranate juice, vinegar, herbs and spices is an age-old combination for making a sweet-and-sour sauce. Liver was traditionally enjoyed with a 'sour sauce', which is really a sweet-and-sour sauce.

 As in this recipe, honey instead of sugar was often used together with vinegar to prepare the sauce.

SERVES: 3

ingredients

500 g lamb's liver

2 Tbsp (30 ml) sunflower oil

1 Tbsp (15 ml) butter

salt and ¼ tsp (1 ml) freshly ground black pepper

1 tsp (5 ml) chopped fresh sage

cake flour, for dusting

2 Tbsp (30 ml) balsamic vinegar

2 Tbsp (30 ml) honey

1 onion, finely minced

6 Tbsp (90 ml) lime juice

2 cups (500 ml) pomegranate or mixed berry juice

1 Tbsp (15 ml) potato flour or cornflour

1 tsp (5 ml) cold water

method

Preheat the oven to 180 °C (350 °F).

Clean the liver thoroughly by removing the thin outer membrane, the arteries and all the glands. Cut into 3 portions.

Heat a frying pan, add the oil and butter and brown the butter.

Season the liver on one side only with the salt and pepper and half the sage. Dust with flour.

Place seasoned side down in a pan and fry for about 4 minutes on one side and about 4 minutes on the other until three-quarters cooked. It must still be slightly pink and just firm to the touch. Remove the liver from the pan and set aside.

Drain any excess fat and deglaze the pan with balsamic vinegar. Add the honey and onion to the pan and cook for 1 minute until golden. Add the lime and pomegranate or mixed berry juices, as well as the remaining sage. Bring to the boil.

Mix the potato flour or cornflour and water and add to the sauce. Cook for 2 minutes until thickened. Add the liver to the sauce and place the pan in the oven for 4 minutes.

Serve with onion rings, mashed potatoes and quince chutney.

SAUCE AND SEASONING

The old Cape recipes for sauces can be divided into seven groups:

- ◢ An olive oil and wine vinegar combination with a little added sugar was the most important sauce or dressing for salad when Jan van Riebeeck came to the Cape in 1652. Depending on the combination, today this sauce is referred to as French or Italian salad dressing. Despite the planting of thousands of olive trees during Jan van Riebeeck's time, the olive harvest was sometimes too poor for pressing sufficient amounts of olive oil and many cooks resorted to using clarified butter (ghee) instead. After the Cape came under British rule for the second time in 1806, only the sugar and vinegar sauce was used, presumably because olive oil was not imported as the British were not fond of eating salad. This sugar and vinegar sauce is still used today to prepare beetroot salad.

- ◢ Various sauces were made to complement meat dishes and this type of sauce was sometimes referred to as ketchup. In his book, *The Oxford Companion to Food*, Alan Davidson views the origin of the word ketchup as from the Chinese *kai-sup* (spiced sauce) or *kêtsiap* (fermented fish sauce). Accordingly, Cape ketchup often contained anchovy. The word ketchup was incorporated by the Dutch into their language and was also used at the Cape. The most well-known ketchup from old Cape cuisine was tomato sauce, which is still widely used today. A unique sweet-and-sour fruit ketchup also developed from pickles, as prepared in Cape kitchens. These sauces, named after the fruit from which they were made, were enjoyed to such an extent by the seventeenth-century slaves at the Cape that they named it *blatjang* (chutney) after the flavouring that was used in their home countries to improve the taste of food. At the beginning of the nineteenth century, Sir Thomas Raffles wrote about *blatjang* in his book *History of Java*. He described it as an Eastern fermented fish sauce that was made from shrimp and small fish and pressed into forms that resembled large cheeses. It had a very strong smell and is still used today as flavouring when preparing food. In Indonesia it was called *trasi* or *terasie* and in Malay *blachang* or *balachan*.

- Sauces such as crayfish and mushroom sauce were useful additions if the taste of certain dishes needed improvement.

- The liquid in which meat was cooked was served with the meal as a sauce to spoon over bread, potatoes and rice. When the sauce needed thickening, finely ground nuts or breadcrumbs were used. In 1651 the French chef La Varennes used a *roux* (paste) to thicken the sauce. He mixed flour with the fat (or butter) in the meat saucepan and added water or stock until it reached the correct consistency.

- Curried sauce for fish and meat curries was already well-known in Europe before Jan van Riebeeck came to the Cape. The slaves called these sauces *kari* or *kerrie* after the chilli sauce they enjoyed with rice in their home countries. By the middle of the eighteenth century, the word *kerrie* started to supersede the names for the old, traditional dishes. The only similarity between the sauce of the slaves and the Cape sauce was that they were both yellow. The Cape curry was made from various spices, of which saffron was essential for flavour and the yellow colour, and it had a meat or fish base. The curry of the slaves consisted of water and chillies, coloured yellow by adding turmeric.

- Egg yolk was sometimes used to thicken the liquid in which food was cooked. The oldest example of such a sauce was prepared by the Roman chef Apicius. He made egg custard by thickening milk with egg yolk. This method was also used by him in the oldest recipe for bobotie (see page 85). During the seventeenth century, this sauce made from milk or the liquid in which meat or vegetables were cooked, together with vinegar, egg and seasoning, was very popular. When the sauce was made with milk it was called white sauce, but when it was made with vinegar or cooking liquid it was called sour sauce – in Britain, sour sauce was called Dutch sauce or Hollandaise. What we know as Hollandaise sauce today was the creation of La Varenne. In 1651 he recorded a recipe in his cookbook for this sour egg sauce with butter.

- The egg custard developed by Apicius was the standard sauce served with desserts until commercial custard powder entered the food products market. Cream was sometimes used instead of custard. Brandy or wine sauce and/or custard was usually served with steamed or baked puddings.

Sour sauce with
slaphakskeentjies

Cape piquant sauce

Mushroom ketchup

Crayfish sauce

Dutch meat and
lemon sauce

Saffron sauce

Cape salad
dressing

Meat sauce with
almonds and ginger

Mushroom powder

Sauces

SOUR SAUCE FOR SLAPHAKSKEENTJIES

This sour sauce wasn't just used for *slaphakskeentjies* (cooked onion salad), but also for green bean salad. The sauce was thickened with egg yolk, but if eggs were in short supply it was thickened with a little flour. Cape mustard, made from the indigenous mustard, was used.

ONIONS
ingredients

1.5 kg pickling onions, peeled but kept whole and with root base intact

method

Place the onions in boiling water, bring back to the boil, and then simmer for 15 minutes until cooked, but not soft. Drain and set aside while you prepare the sauce.

SOUR SAUCE
ingredients

1 tsp (5 ml) salt

1 Tbsp (15 ml) mustard powder

1 cup (250 ml) sugar

1½ Tbsp (22.5 ml) cornflour

5 eggs, beaten

⅔ cup (160 ml) wine vinegar

1¼ cups (300 ml) water

1 cup (250 ml) fresh cream (optional, and can be substituted with water)

method

Mix the salt, mustard, sugar and cornflour together.

Add the eggs and whisk well until lump free.

Mix the vinegar and water. Add to the egg mixture, whisking continuously. Add the cream or water.

Pour the mixture into the top of a double-boiler (or place in a heatproof bowl over simmering water), stirring until it thickens.

Pour the sauce over the onions and serve chilled, or bottle in sterilised jars.

Photograph on page 139

DUTCH MEAT AND LEMON SAUCE

This sauce goes particularly well with grilled meat.

ingredients

2 cups (500 ml) lamb stock (see recipe on page 243)

1 sprig fresh rosemary, picked and chopped

1 Tbsp (15 ml) finely grated lemon zest

pinch of ground cinnamon

blade of mace or pinch of grated nutmeg

10 black peppercorns

3 egg yolks

1 tsp (5 ml) vinegar

1½ Tbsp (22.5 ml) lemon juice

250 g butter, melted, clarified and kept warm

salt

method

Place the stock, rosemary, lemon zest, cinnamon, mace or nutmeg and peppercorns in a saucepan and cook until reduced by three-quarters to a thick glaze. Keep warm.

Place the egg yolks, vinegar and lemon juice in a metal bowl and beat.

Place the bowl over a pot of boiling water and whisk while adding the meat glaze.

Whisk until the sauce is thickened enough to coat the back of a wooden spoon, and then remove from the heat.

Slowly whisk in the clarified butter and season with salt to taste. Serve immediately.

Photograph on page 139

Meat sauce with almonds and ginger

MAKES: 500 ml

During the seventeenth and eighteenth centuries, nuts were used extensively in the preparation of meat and baked products. This recipe is a typical example of a sauce that dates from that period. The sauce was thickened with finely ground almonds and a pinch of sugar was usually added as seasoning. Serve with poultry or venison.

ingredients

4 cups (1 litre) veal or beef stock (see recipe on page 243)

1 tsp (5 ml) sugar

pinch of saffron

2 tsp (10 ml) minced fresh root ginger

½ cup (125 ml) toasted flaked almonds, chopped

pinch of grated nutmeg

¼ tsp (1 ml) lemon zest

2 egg yolks

1 tsp (5 ml) lemon juice, plus additional for seasoning

salt and freshly ground black pepper

½ tsp (2.5 ml) finely chopped fresh parsley

method

Place the stock, sugar, saffron, ginger, almonds, nutmeg and lemon zest in a saucepan, bring to the boil and reduce by half. Let it cool slightly (to prevent the egg yolks from curdling when the stock is added).

Place the egg yolks and lemon juice in a bowl, beat together, and then add 3 Tbsp (45 ml) of the hot stock. Beat until thickened, and then add this mixture to the remaining stock, beating continuously.

Cook over low heat until thick and season to taste with salt, pepper and lemon juice – do not let it come to the boil after you've added the egg. Stir in the parsley and serve immediately.

Photograph on page 139

Crayfish sauce

MAKES: 300 ml

Mary Sanderson's cookbook (1770) features many unusual recipes, of which this one grabs the attention immediately. According to her, this sauce can be kept for up to three years. It is a 100 per cent natural taste enhancer — much better than today's synthetic versions. Use spoonfuls of it in soup, pasta or curries, especially fish curry, for a unique taste experience.

ingredients

2 cups (2 x 250 ml) crayfish shells

¼ cup (60 ml) sunflower oil

4 cups (1 litre) water

1 cup (250 ml) sugar

4 blades mace or 1 Tbsp (15 ml) grated nutmeg

½ tsp (2.5 ml) ground cloves

6 anchovy fillets, pounded to a paste

1 cup (250 ml) sherry

½ cup (125 ml) wine vinegar

1 tsp (5 ml) cumin seeds, roasted

1 sprig fresh rosemary, finely chopped

method

Put the crayfish shells and oil in a heavy-based saucepan and leave it on high heat until the shells almost burn. Add the water and simmer for 20 minutes.

Remove the crayfish shells with a slotted spoon and work the shells in a food processor with a little of the cooking liquid until finely chopped. Return the chopped mixture to the saucepan and simmer 10 minutes longer.

Strain the mixture through a fine sieve and return the liquid to the saucepan. Add the sugar and stir until dissolved.

Add the rest of the ingredients and simmer slowly until reduced to 300 ml.

Place in a sterilised container and store in the refrigerator.

Photograph on page 139

NOTE:

Mary also writes that the sauce must be 'shaken and strained before use'.

Cape mayonnaise

The history of the development of mayonnaise is uncertain. Anne Willan gives a plausible explanation for the origins of mayonnaise in her book *Great Cooks and Their Recipes*, where she reasons that it originated in France as the name could have come from the Old French for egg yolk (*moyeu*).

MAKES: just over 2 cups (600 ml)

ingredients

3 egg yolks

1 Tbsp (15 ml) lemon juice

1 tsp (5 ml) Dijon mustard

pinch of sugar

¼ tsp (1 ml) salt

pinch of saffron (optional)

1 tsp (5 ml) vinegar

2 cups (500 ml) vegetable oil

method

Place the egg yolks, lemon juice, mustard, sugar, salt, saffron (if using) and vinegar in a bowl and whisk well.

Slowly trickle in the oil while beating vigorously. Make sure to add the oil very slowly for the first 7 Tbsp (105 ml) to ensure a stable emulsion.

If the mayonnaise is too thick, add a few drops of water right at the end to thin it out.

The mayonnaise will keep for up to 1 week in the refrigerator.

Mushroom ketchup

This recipe was found in an eighteenth-century Cape cookbook and has been adapted for the modern palate. Serve with grilled steak or roast beef.

ingredients

4 medium onions

2 Tbsp (30 ml) coarse sea salt

3 Tbsp (45 ml) olive or sunflower oil

1 kg field mushrooms or brown mushrooms, chopped

½ cup (125 ml) balsamic vinegar

¾ cup (190 ml) red wine vinegar

1 cup (250 ml) sweet sherry

1 Tbsp (15 ml) brown sugar

1 Tbsp (15 ml) honey

1 sprig fresh thyme

1 sprig fresh marjoram

1 tsp (5 ml) ground allspice

1 tsp (5 ml) ground coriander

½ tsp (2.5 ml) freshly ground black pepper

1 tsp (5 ml) smoked paprika (optional)

2 tsp (10 ml) chopped anchovy fillets

method

Preheat the oven to 180 °C (350 °F).

Place the onions on the coarse sea salt on a tray and roast for about 20 minutes until tender. Chop finely and set aside.

Heat a large saucepan, add the oil and cook the mushrooms over high heat for 3 minutes.

Add the remaining ingredients, including the onions, and cook for 30 minutes over low heat.

Blend or chop the mixture coarsely, return to the saucepan and reduce until thick.

Place in sterilised jars.

Photograph on page 139

Green walnut pickle

ingredients

1.5 kg green walnuts

125 g salt

7 cups (1.75 litres) water

25 g black peppercorns

1 tsp (5 ml) allspice berries

5 cups (1.25 litres) wine vinegar

5 cups (5 x 250 ml) sugar

1 Tbsp (15 ml) mustard seeds

1 tsp (5 ml) grated fresh root ginger

1 large cinnamon stick, crushed

method

Prick the walnuts all over with a large needle (the walnuts must be picked while the insides are still soft). Place the nuts in a ceramic bowl, dissolve half the salt in half the water and pour over the walnuts. Cover and leave for 5 days in a cool place, stirring twice a day to ensure even brining.

Drain the walnuts, mix the remaining salt and water, pour over the walnuts and leave for another 5 days, stirring twice a day as before. Drain, spread out in a single layer in a flat dish or on a tray and dry in the sun until they are black but not dry, turning every few hours.

Crush the peppercorns and allspice berries and simmer in the vinegar with the sugar and spices for 20 minutes. Leave to cool and then strain.

Pack the walnuts into sterilised, wide-mouth jars, filling them no more than three-quarters full. Pour in the spiced vinegar, cover and leave in a cool place for 6 weeks before using.

CAPE PIQUANT SAUCE

MAKES: 2 cups (500 ml)

This is not an easy sauce to prepare if you don't already have the walnut pickle and mushroom ketchup, but it is included here because it is such an interesting recipe. It was found in Mary Sanderson's Cape cookbook, where she lists the ingredients but does not include the method. She does mention, though, that the bottle has to be shaken before use.

This sauce was probably used as a condiment at the table, in the same manner as Worcestershire sauce is used today.

During the late seventeenth and eighteenth centuries, walnut trees were in abundance on farms where there was enough water. Whole green walnut jam was a popular treat served with tea in the afternoon.

ingredients

1 cup (250 ml) walnut pickle (see recipe on opposite page) or 1 can (560 g) water chestnuts, drained

1 cup (250 ml) mushroom ketchup (see recipe on opposite page)

1 tsp (5 ml) chopped anchovy fillets

1 clove garlic, chopped

¼ tsp (1 ml) cayenne pepper

sugar to taste (optional)

method

Blend all the ingredients together until smooth. Place in a saucepan, bring to the boil and simmer for 10 minutes.

Place in a sterilised jar.

Photograph on page 139

CAPE SALAD DRESSING

MAKES: 1½ cups (375 ml)

This salad dressing is based on an old Roman recipe. Instead of adding the finely grated egg to the dressing, the eggs were sometimes halved and arranged on top of the lettuce with onion rings, before the salad dressing was poured over.

ingredients

3 hard-boiled egg yolks, finely grated

1 Tbsp (15 ml) mustard powder

salt and freshly ground black pepper

1 tsp (5 ml) honey

1 tsp (5 ml) brown sugar

2 Tbsp (30 ml) wine vinegar or flavoured vinegar of your choice

½ cup (125 ml) vegetable oil

½ tsp (2.5 ml) chopped fresh oregano

method

Place the egg yolks, mustard powder and seasoning in a bowl. Set aside.

Place the honey, sugar and vinegar in a saucepan over medium heat and stir until the sugar dissolves. Leave to cool before whisking into the egg yolk mixture.

Gradually whisk in the oil and lastly season with oregano, salt and pepper to taste.

Photograph on page 139

SAFFRON SAUCE

The idea for this sauce was inspired by C. Louis Leipoldt's recipe, in his book titled *Leipoldt's Food and Wine*. According to him, the sauce recipe is very old, but Leipoldt doesn't list his sources.

Even though turmeric was grown at the Cape, most cooks from the seventeenth century and even well into the eighteenth and nineteenth centuries preferred using saffron. It was more expensive than pepper, but because it was also cultivated at the Cape it probably wasn't beyond the reach of cooks from wealthy households. This is a sublime sauce to serve with game, pork or smoked tongue.

ingredients

2 tsp (10 ml) butter

1 onion, chopped

1 clove garlic

1 tsp (5 ml) brown sugar

flesh of 1 baked quince (can substitute with flesh of 2 baked Granny Smith apples), puréed

pinch of saffron

2 cups (500 ml) veal stock (see recipe on page 243)

extra 2 Tbsp (30 ml) butter

salt and freshly ground black pepper

method

Melt the butter in a saucepan and sweat the onion, garlic and sugar until the onion is soft.

Add the quince or apple purée, saffron and half the stock. Cook for 10 minutes. Add the rest of the stock, cook for a few minutes and then pass through a sieve.

Whisk in the extra butter and season to taste with salt and pepper.

Photograph on page 139

MUSHROOM POWDER

At the Cape, when wild mushrooms were plentiful, they were picked and preserved in a spiced sauce or dried for later use. Cooks used their own preferred herbs and spices to improve the taste of the mushrooms. Add to soups, pastas, sauces or vegetables to enhance the flavour.

ingredients

1 kg field mushrooms or brown mushrooms

salt, for sprinkling

1 tsp (5 ml) grated nutmeg

1 tsp (5 ml) ground cloves

1 Tbsp (15 ml) freshly ground black pepper

4 Tbsp (60 ml) coarse sea salt

2 Tbsp (30 ml) dried thyme

2 Tbsp (30 ml) dried rosemary

method

Preheat the oven to 100 °C (200 °F).

Peel and scrape the mushrooms very clean. Cut into 3 mm thick slices. Set them in an earthenware dish, sprinkle a little salt over them and bake overnight.

The following day, pour off the liquid and return the mushrooms to the oven until they are dry enough to powder – another 12 hours.

In a food processor, powder the mushrooms with the nutmeg, cloves and pepper. Mix with the coarse sea salt, thyme and rosemary.

If you prefer, you can process it all together to a powder, but we prefer it coarser with more texture.

Photograph on page 139

VEGETABLES AND SALADS

Jan van Riebeeck's Company's Garden must have been a feast for the eyes back in the late-1600s. The pastor Valentyn compares it with the exquisite ancient gardens of Hesperides and the hanging gardens of Babylon. According to him, the Company's Garden was the most beautiful of them all. Valentyn further writes that he had never seen such large onions, cauliflowers, cabbages and quinces anywhere else. Jan van Riebeeck's love for gardening is clearly evident from his elaborate journal entries and the almanac for gardeners and farmers he left behind for his successor.

The complete list of vegetables and fruit planted in the Company's Garden is impressive. Herbs such as thyme, parsley, oregano, marjoram, basil, rosemary, celery, coriander, fennel, borage, savory, catnip, veronica and pimpernel, which was part of the food culture before the British colonised the Cape in 1806, were in abundance. Nuts such as chestnuts, walnuts, hazelnuts, almonds (hard and soft husk) and pistachios (also called green almonds) were also available in the Company's Garden and part of daily cooking.

Because the Netherlands is a small country and couldn't produce enough meat at that time, vegetables were always important in the food culture of the Dutch. The Cape was therefore more advanced than many countries regarding the large variety of vegetables available for preparing tasty dishes. With this abundance of fruit and vegetables available, there was a certain status afforded to serving several vegetable dishes. Lady Anne Barnard, whose husband was the secretary to Governor McCartney at the end of the eighteenth century, mentioned that there were even up to eight vegetable dishes served at the dinner table.

Sweet-and-sour peas

Dried peas were considered a staple food in Europe for centuries. During the sixteenth century, the Dutch developed sugar peas and introduced shelled, fresh green peas to the rest of the world.
  During Jan van Riebeeck's time at the Cape in the seventeenth century, people were already enjoying the fabulous taste of green peas, while it only became fashionable in France at the end of that century.
  Young green peas in the pod were used in salads or lightly cooked. Shelled green peas were traditionally prepared as a sweet dish and sometimes dumplings were cooked on top of the peas.

SERVES: 4–6

ingredients

1 onion, chopped

½ tsp (2.5 ml) chopped fresh
root ginger

1 tsp (5 ml) cooking oil

2 Tbsp (30 ml) honey

2 Tbsp (30 ml) vinegar

¼ tsp (1 ml) grated nutmeg

pinch of ground cinnamon

1 tsp (5 ml) sweet mustard

½ cup (125 ml) fresh cream
(optional)

2 cups (500 ml) shelled fresh peas

method

Heat a pan and sweat the onion and ginger in the oil. Add the honey, vinegar, spices and mustard. Add the cream (if using) and cook until thick. Remove from the heat and leave to cool.

Simmer the peas in boiling water for just over a minute until tender, and then refresh in iced water.

Drain the peas and mix with the sauce.

Serve hot or cold.

Cape vegetable stew

This dish is based on a recipe from a Dutch cookbook from the Middle Ages called *Wel ende edelike spijse*. As was common in many of the old recipes, wine, a little sugar and spices were used generously in the dish. The sugar was usually seen as a spice and therefore only a little was used.

SERVES: 6

ingredients

2 Tbsp (30 ml) olive oil

2 onions, sliced

2 fennel bulbs, thinly sliced

1 Tbsp (15 ml) chopped fresh root ginger

2 cloves garlic, chopped

1 cup (250 ml) sliced cabbage

¼ cup (60 ml) vinegar

6 artichoke hearts, cleaned

2 cups (500 ml) peeled baby carrots

1 cup (250 ml) sorrel, chopped

2 cups (500 ml) chopped spinach

2 cups (500 ml) cubed ripe pumpkin

1 cup (250 ml) white wine

2 Tbsp (30 ml) brown sugar

1 Tbsp (15 ml) chopped fresh thyme

pinch of ground cinnamon

pinch of ground allspice

2 cups (500 ml) vegetable *nage* (see recipe on page 242)

salt and freshly ground black pepper

method

Heat the oil in a stovetop casserole dish or saucepan and sweat the onions, fennel, ginger, garlic and cabbage.

Add the vinegar and artichoke hearts, fit the lid and steam for 5 minutes (to prevent the artichokes from discolouring).

Add the remaining ingredients and stew until the sauce thickens and all the ingredients are tender.

Serve with lentils or rice.

Asparagus
and goat's cheese soufflé

The ancient Greeks and Romans used asparagus. It was cultivated in the Netherlands during the fourteenth century and Van Riebeeck planted it in the Company's garden at the Cape. From June 1652 until the cultivated variety could be harvested, the Dutch used the roots and thin new shoots of the wild asparagus at the Cape. Wild asparagus remained popular among some people until the end of the nineteenth century, as it had an excellent flavour and was available when the garden type was out of season.

Asparagus was always lightly cooked by the seventeenth and eighteenth century cooks of the Cape. It was used in various dishes, such as salads, soups, *bredies* and tarts. As a dish on its own, it was served with melted butter and a sprinkling of nutmeg or with a garnish of finely chopped hard-boiled egg yolks and parsley. It was also served with sour egg sauce or Hollandaise.

SERVES: 10

ingredients

2 Tbsp (30 ml) soft butter

1 cup (250 ml) dried breadcrumbs

6 Tbsp (90 ml) butter

6 Tbsp (90 ml) cake flour

2 cups (500 ml) goat's milk

200 g soft goat's cheese

100 g goat's pecorino cheese

½ cup (125 ml) cooked and chopped asparagus

1 tsp (5 ml) salt

½ tsp (2.5 ml) ground white pepper

5 egg yolks

6 egg whites

method

Preheat the oven to 180 °C (350 °F).

Butter 10 x 100–150 ml moulds (6 cm diameter, and 6 cm deep) and dust with the breadcrumbs. Place in the refrigerator to harden.

Melt the 6 Tbsp (90 ml) butter and add the flour. Cook for 5 minutes over low heat. Gradually add the milk and cook for about 12 minutes until the mixture doesn't taste floury.

Remove from the heat and beat in the cheeses and asparagus. Leave to cool slightly.

Season well, add the egg yolks and beat in.

Whisk the egg whites until stiff and fold into the cheese sauce.

Spoon the mixture into the moulds and place the moulds in an oven pan on top of a cloth.

Pour hot water into the pan, making sure to reach at least a quarter way up the moulds and bake for 20 minutes – do not open the oven.

Remove the soufflés – they should be firm to the touch – and leave to cool for 15 minutes before unmoulding.

Serve with Pickled Beetroot (see recipe on page 171) and a sorrel and rocket salad.

NOTE:
These soufflés can be made ahead and stored in the fridge.
Reheat at 180 °C (350 °F) for 8–10 minutes.

Potato salad

Potato and turnip
dauphinoise

Sweetcorn fritters

Sweetcorn fritters

In the Cape cuisine of the seventeenth and eighteenth centuries, almost any vegetable, fish or meat was processed into a fritter. Pumpkin fritters are still well-known and popular, but potato, sweet potato, apricot and peach fritters in the tradition of this recipe have fallen out of favour.

SERVES: 4

ingredients

2 cups (500 ml) cake flour

2 Tbsp (30 ml) baking powder

pinch of grated nutmeg

pinch of cayenne pepper

½ tsp (2.5 ml) salt

1 Tbsp (15 ml) chopped fresh basil

2 spring onions, chopped

just over 1½ cups (400 ml) milk

2 cups (500 ml) sweetcorn kernels
(blanched and cut off the cob)

sunflower oil, for shallow frying

method

Sift the flour and baking powder together. Add the nutmeg, cayenne pepper, salt, basil and spring onions.

Whisk in the milk and add the sweetcorn kernels. Set aside for 1 hour, then give the mixture another stir.

Fry tablespoonfuls in shallow oil in a frying pan, turning once, until golden brown. Remove from the pan and drain excess oil on paper towel.

Potato salad

Potatoes in one form or another should feature at any good barbecue or picnic. This variation on potato salad consists of ingredients that were readily available during Jan van Riebeeck's time at the Cape. It is a superb dish that can even be enjoyed as a meal on its own.

SERVES: 4

ingredients

1 kg baby potatoes, scrubbed (do not peel)

1 Tbsp (15 ml) butter

pinch of saffron

1 Tbsp (15 ml) coarse sea salt

4–8 cups (1–2 litres) vegetable stock (see recipe on page 242)

3 artichokes, cooked and sliced in half

butter and olive oil

1 cup (250 ml) porcini or field mushrooms, sliced

1 small onion, chopped

pinch of chopped garlic

pinch of lemon zest

1 bunch thin asparagus

2 tsp (10 ml) balsamic vinegar

2 Tbsp (30 ml) sour cream

1 tsp (5 ml) snipped chives

1 cup (250 ml) sorrel

¼ cup (60 ml) Parmesan cheese shavings

method

Place the potatoes, butter, saffron, salt and stock in a saucepan. Cover the surface with parchment (baking) paper and simmer very slowly for about 25 minutes until tender.

Peel the potatoes carefully while still hot and return them to the cooking liquid. Leave to cool in the liquid to absorb the colour from the saffron.

Reheat the potatoes in the same liquid.

Toss the artichokes in olive oil and grill for 2–3 minutes.

Heat a saucepan with olive oil and butter. Add the mushrooms, onion, garlic, lemon zest and asparagus and cook for 2 minutes.

Remove from the heat and strain off all the fat. Add the balsamic vinegar, sour cream and artichokes.

Remove the potatoes from the hot liquid and toss in a bowl with the chives and some sea salt. Place on a plate and spoon the vegetables in sour cream around them. Top with the sorrel and Parmesan shavings.

Photograph on page 154

Potato and turnip
dauphinoise

At the end of the fifteenth century, when the Spanish brought the first potatoes from America to Europe, many people refused to eat them because they belonged to the same family as the deadly nightshade. However, in the nineteenth century potatoes replaced turnips as the most popular vegetable in Europe. The first potatoes at the Cape were planted during Van Riebeeck's time.

SERVES: 8–10

ingredients

1 cup (250 ml) honey

2 sprigs fresh rosemary

4 cups (1 litre) fresh cream

4 cloves garlic

2 bay leaves

1 tsp (5 ml) black peppercorns

butter or lamb's fat

6 large turnips, peeled and thinly sliced

6 medium potatoes, peeled and thinly sliced

1 cup (250 ml) freshly grated Parmesan cheese

3 cloves garlic, finely chopped

salt and freshly ground black pepper

½ cup (125 ml) fresh breadcrumbs, for topping

½ cup (125 ml) freshly grated Parmesan cheese, for topping

(optional: diced bacon, sautéed and sprinkled in-between layers)

method

Place the honey and rosemary in a saucepan and cook until the honey starts to caramelise.

Add the cream, garlic, bay leaves and peppercorns and bring to the boil. Remove from the heat and leave in a warm place to infuse for 1 hour. Strain through a sieve.

Preheat the oven to 180 °C (350 °F). Grease an ovenproof dish with butter or lamb's fat.

Place one layer of turnips in the ovenproof dish, followed by a layer of potatoes. Top with a layer of Parmesan and garlic and season with salt and pepper.

Repeat this process until you've used all the turnips, potatoes and cheese. Pour the cream sauce over. Place a piece of greaseproof paper on the surface of the dauphinoise and place in the oven. Bake until the turnips and potatoes are tender, about 45 minutes. Remove the paper and return to the oven until the sauce has reduced by three-quarters and the dauphinoise is golden brown.

Leave to cool for 2 hours. Place a weight on top and refrigerate for at least 6 hours before use.

Cut into squares, sprinkle with a mixture of breadcrumbs and cheese and place in a hot oven to gratinate. Serve with roasted venison, pickled red cabbage and a Shiraz jus.

Photograph on page 154

Pumpkin tart

with curried mango sorbet

Pumpkin tart used to be popular at the Cape, but it lost its popularity after British colonisation. The Dutch had also taken the recipe to America, where pumpkin pie is a national dish today. Sorbet as in this recipe wasn't prepared at the Cape because of the climate and the unavailability of refrigeration until the twentieth century.

SERVES: 10–12

PUMPKIN PURÉE
ingredients

1 kg pumpkin, diced

30 g fresh root ginger, chopped

70 g butter

1 tsp (5 ml) salt

method

Place all the purée ingredients in a saucepan, cover with a lid and cook until soft. Purée until smooth.

PASTRY
ingredients

250 g cake flour

125 g ground walnuts

½ tsp (2.5 ml) ground ginger

½ tsp (2.5 ml) grated nutmeg

½ tsp (2.5 ml) ground cinnamon

1 egg

½ tsp (2.5 ml) smoked salt

150 g butter

method

Preheat the oven to 180 °C (350 °F).

Place all the pastry ingredients in a food processor and work into a paste.

Roll out on a lightly floured surface and use it to line a greased 24 cm tart mould. Use a sharp knife to trim the pastry level with the rim of the tart mould. Place a layer of parchment (baking) paper inside the mould, fill with dried beans and bake blind for 15 minutes.

FILLING
ingredients

3½ cups (875 ml) pumpkin purée

½ cup (125 ml) sugar

1 cup (250 ml) cake flour

2 tsp (10 ml) baking powder

3 eggs

1 egg yolk

1 cup (250 ml) fresh cream

1 cup (250 ml) milk

3 Tbsp (45 ml) butter

method

Set the oven temperature to 130 °C (265 °F).

Place all the filling ingredients, except the butter, in a mixing bowl and whisk until incorporated.

Melt the butter in a hot pan and cook until brown and fragrant. Add to the filling mixture and whisk.

Pour the filling into the baked tart mould, tap lightly on a hard surface to remove any air bubbles, and bake for 40 minutes until set.

DECORATION
ingredients

2 pieces crystallised ginger, julienned

¼ cup (60 ml) icing sugar

method

Cut the pumpkin tart into wedges. For a starter, serve hot or at room temperature on a dinner plate with a scoop of Curried Mango Sorbet, a thin slice of crystallised ginger and a dusting of icing sugar. If you wish to serve this as a dessert, sprinkle the tart with cinnamon sugar and serve with a scoop of ice cream instead of the sorbet.

Photograph on page 161

CURRIED MANGO SORBET
ingredients

2 bay leaves

½ tsp (2.5 ml) coriander seeds

5 whole cloves

2 onions, chopped

1 Tbsp (15 ml) curry mix 2
(see recipe on page 248)

1 cup (250 ml) white wine vinegar

½ cup (125 ml) brown sugar

1 tsp (5 ml) turmeric

1 tsp (5 ml) salt

1 fresh red chilli

750 g fresh or canned mango flesh, cubed or sliced

½ cucumber, diced and frozen

method

Tie the bay leaves, coriander and cloves in a muslin bag. Place the bag and the remaining ingredients, except the mango and cucumber, in a large, heavy-based saucepan. Bring to the boil and reduce until syrupy.

Remove from the heat and discard the spice bag. Add the mango and cucumber.

Transfer the mixture to a blender and blend until smooth. Chill in an ice-cream maker until frozen.

If you do not have an ice-cream maker, first purée the mixture and then place it in a freezerproof container. Take it out of the freezer every hour and whisk until the ice crystals are broken up. Continue with this procedure until completely frozen.

Sweet potatoes

with *moskonfyt* (must jam)

Sweet potatoes were planted by Jan van Riebeeck at the Cape and were usually baked or cooked whole, mashed or cut up and stewed with sugar, cinnamon or naartjie peel and butter.

SERVES: 4

ingredients

4 medium sweet potatoes, scrubbed

¼ cup (60 ml) *moskonfyt*
or use cinnamon sugar

¼ cup (60 ml) butter

method

Preheat the oven to 180 °C (350 °F).

Place the sweet potatoes on a baking tray and roast for 45–60 minutes.

Remove from the oven and squeeze the sweet potatoes until they burst open. Drizzle with *moskonfyt* or cinnamon sugar and butter and serve as an accompaniment to roasts or braaied snoek.

Steamed artichokes
with fennel

In Van Riebeeck's time, artichokes were in abundance at the Cape and used in many recipes.

SERVES: 8

ingredients

2 Tbsp (30 ml) olive oil

2 onions, thinly sliced

2 fennel bulbs, thinly sliced

4 cloves garlic, sliced

2 sprigs fresh thyme

1 tsp (5 ml) mustard seeds

1 tsp (5 ml) ground coriander

½ tsp (2.5 ml) freshly ground
black pepper

½ tsp (2.5 ml) grated nutmeg

2 Tbsp (30 ml) sugar

½ cup (125 ml) vinegar

½ cup (125 ml) dry white wine

8 artichokes, cleaned and placed in
lemon water

4 cups (1 litre) vegetable *nage* (stock)
(see recipe on page 242)

salt and freshly ground
black pepper

method

Heat a stovetop casserole dish or saucepan, add the olive oil and sweat
the onions, fennel, garlic and thyme for 5 minutes.

Add the mustard seeds, spices, sugar, vinegar and wine. Place the
artichokes on top and steam with the lid on for 5 minutes to retain
good colour.

Add the vegetable *nage*, season with salt and pepper to taste and cook
for 15–20 minutes until the sauce is thick and the artichokes tender.
Check seasoning.

Cape mixed salad

ingredients

500 g mixed salad leaves

½ cup (125 ml) baby green beans, blanched

3 hard-boiled eggs, halved or cut into wedges

4 radishes, thinly sliced

½ red onion, thinly sliced

¼ cup (60 ml) thinly sliced fennel bulb

¼ cup (60 ml) vinegar

8 Tbsp (120 ml) olive oil

salt and freshly ground black pepper

method

Arrange the salad leaves on a large salad platter. Layer the beans, boiled eggs, radishes, onion and fennel on top.

Mix the vinegar and olive oil together, season to taste and sprinkle over the salad just before serving.

Cucumber salad

This old Cape salad consists of cucumber, onions, anchovy, vinegar and a pinch of cayenne pepper.

Graters for nutmeg were used early on at the Cape, but vegetable graters were only available from the nineteenth century, therefore vegetables and fruit for salad were usually finely chopped.

SERVES: 4–6

ingredients

1 cucumber, coarsely grated or finely chopped

sea salt flakes

pinch of cayenne pepper

2 spring onions, finely chopped

1 anchovy fillet, chopped

2 tsp (10 ml) sherry vinegar

3 Tbsp (45 ml) olive oil

pinch of sugar

method

Sprinkle the cucumber with the salt and cayenne pepper.

Toss the rest of the ingredients together, mix with the cucumber and place in a serving bowl.

Serve immediately.

Photograph on page 84

NOTE:

Add 1 can (410 g) mango chunks or 1 fresh mango, cubed, for variation.

vegetables and salads

Pickled beetroot

This recipe was found in an eighteenth-century Cape cookbook. The inclusion of ginger and horseradish is an interesting combination, as pickled beetroot today usually only consists of beetroot, vinegar and sugar. Horseradish was an important ingredient in old Cape cuisine, but today very few people still know and use it.

SERVES: 10—12

ingredients

2 star anise

3 whole cloves

2 whole allspice

2½ cups (625 ml) vinegar

3 cups (750 ml) sugar

¼ tsp (1 ml) peeled and chopped fresh root ginger, or to taste

¼ tsp (1 ml) peeled and chopped fresh horseradish, or to taste

5 bunches medium beetroot, cooked until just tender and peeled while still warm

method

Place all the spices in a muslin bag and secure with a piece of string.

Heat the spices with the vinegar, sugar, ginger and horseradish in a saucepan, stirring until the sugar has dissolved. Bring to the boil.

Add the cubed, sliced or grated beetroot (your preference) and heat until boiling.

Remove the spice bag and squeeze all the liquid from it. Pour the pickle into sterilised jars or into an airtight container and refrigerate.

Sambals

Sambals is the name used by the slaves for the finely chopped salads of the Cape.

Cucumber and bean

SERVES: 4–6

This sambal goes particularly well with curried dishes.

ingredients

2 hard-boiled eggs

2 Tbsp (30 ml) vinegar

1 tsp (5 ml) mustard powder

½ tsp (2.5 ml) lemon grass, pounded to a paste

1 tsp (5 ml) sugar

½ fresh red chilli, chopped

⅓ cup (80 ml) vegetable oil

1 cucumber, peeled and thinly sliced

450 g cooked green beans, chopped

salt and freshly ground black pepper

method

Finely grate the eggs and mix in the vinegar, mustard powder, lemon grass, sugar, chilli and oil.

Mix with the cucumber and beans and season to taste.

Photograph on page 80

Beetroot and horseradish

SERVES: 4–6

ingredients

1 cup (250 ml) grated or diced cooked or roasted beetroot

1 Tbsp (15 ml) finely chopped fresh horseradish or 2 Tbsp (30 ml) ready-made horseradish

1 Tbsp (15 ml) sour cream

2 spring onions, sliced

1 Tbsp (15 ml) snipped chives

pinch of ground cloves

1 tsp (5 ml) lemon juice

salt and freshly ground black pepper to taste

method

Mix all the ingredients together well and serve chilled.

Photograph on page 80

Lentil sambal

An ideal accompaniment to a curry.

ingredients

1 Tbsp (15 ml) olive oil

2 onions, chopped

½ cup (125 ml) chopped spring onions, including green parts

½ tsp (2.5 ml) chopped garlic

½ tsp (2.5 ml) chopped fresh root ginger

1 Tbsp (15 ml) diced baby carrot

1 Tbsp (15 ml) diced celery

2 tsp (10 ml) curry mix 2 (see recipe on page 78)

pinch of saffron

1 cup (250 ml) water

½ cup (125 ml) milk

½ cup (125 ml) dried red lentils

1 tsp (5 ml) chopped fresh coriander

salt and freshly ground black pepper

method

Heat the oil in a large saucepan and sauté the onions, spring onions, garlic, ginger, carrot and celery.

Add the curry mix and saffron and sauté for 2 minutes.

Add the water, milk and lentils and cook until soft and thick – cooking times vary so keep an eye on them otherwise you'll end up with a soupy, lentil mush.

Leave to cool and then add the coriander. Season to taste.

Photograph on page 80

Quince sambal

ingredients

3 ripe quinces, peeled and chopped

¼ onion, finely chopped

1 fresh green chilli, chopped (optional)

¼ tsp (1 ml) coarse salt

sugar to taste

method

Pound all the ingredients to a paste and serve with venison or *sult*.

Pasta

The ancient Persians were already cooking a form of pasta many hundreds of years ago. Judging from an Arabian recipe in *A Baghdad Cookery Book* (1226) translated by Charles Berry, it seems as if the pasta dough only contained flour and water and no eggs, with air as the leavening agent kneaded into the dough. The dough was then thinly rolled out, left for a while to dry off, and then cut up into equally broad strips that were dusted well with flour and placed on top of each other. These strips were further cut up into such fine strips that the Arabs called it *rishta* meaning 'hair'. These noodles were used in soup. This Arabian method for making pasta was still followed by many South Africans up until the twentieth century, when it was used in soup and traditional *melkkos* (milk food), which was also known as *melksnysels* (milk noodles).

The earliest reference to homemade pasta at the Cape is the list compiled in 1754 by Von Dessin, a former Master at the Cape, when he took stock of the contents of his pantry and listed *laxa* among the items. He didn't assign weight to this product as he did for the other things on his list, which indicates that it was homemade dried pasta. Charles Perry mentions in his *Notes on Persian Pasta* (in Maxime Rodison et al., *Medieval Arab Cookery*, 2001) that *laxa* was an abbreviation of the Persian word *lakhsha*, which describes the slipperiness of cooked noodles. The Yiddish word for it is *lokshn* from the Ukrainian *lokshina*.

At the end of the eighteenth century, Lady Anne Barnard indirectly referred to Cape homemade pasta when she declared that she will from now on also serve 'macaroni, tarts, puddings or such things ...' at her dinner table. The macaroni (from the Italian *maccheroni*) Lady Anne mentioned, was probably a machine-made product that was introduced to the market at that time. This shop-bought product became so popular during the nineteenth century that very few cooks still made their own, although the homemade pasta was tastier than the ready-made product. The old name *snysels* (noodles) had to make way for macaroni and lasagne, and the shop-bought product that resembled *laxa* became known as vermicelli.

Machines for making pasta became available during the twentieth century, which made producing pasta a lot easier, as it took a whole day otherwise. The dough had to be kneaded for a long time before rolling it out thinly until it had the appearance of chamois leather. Because it required so much effort, large quantities were usually made, which were then hung up to dry over a stick and later stored in airtight containers.

Ravioli

with wild mushrooms and goat's cheese

Persian-Arabian pasta recipes were also known in Spain, but it was the Italians who experimented with the recipes and exported the use of pasta to France. The Italian cooks started to fold pieces of meat or vegetables into pasta dough strips, which they then fried in fat. According to Anne Willan (*Great Cooks and Their Recipes*), they called this dish *rabiole*, which means 'leftover' in the Ligurian dialect. In the recipes of the Italian chef Martino (1474), pieces of pasta dough were filled with spiced meat, which were then cooked in saffron water. He called this dish *ravioli* and served it with cheese and cinnamon sugar. In his cookbook *Opera* (1570), the Italian chef Scappi gave a variation on pasta dough that contained eggs. Today, eggs are mainly used when preparing pasta dough for cooking ravioli.

The Dutch, who traded in the Mediterranean, took these Italian recipes to the Netherlands, where they developed their own fillings. Proof of this development is a ravioli recipe with a cheese filling that appears in Thomas van der Noot's cookbook (1510). These recipes also made their way to the Cape when the Dutch settled here.

SERVES: 6

ingredients

2 Tbsp (30 ml) olive oil

1 Tbsp (15 ml) butter

500 g mixed field mushrooms or brown mushrooms

2 cloves garlic

1 knob fresh root ginger, peeled and finely chopped

salt and freshly ground black pepper

1 Tbsp (15 ml) chopped fresh oregano

¼ cup (60 ml) grated Parmesan cheese

½ cup (125 ml) goat's chèvre cheese

1 spring onion, chopped

¼ quantity basic pasta dough 1 (see recipe on page 249)

beaten egg or water, for brushing

chopped spring onions and grated Parmesan cheese, for serving

olive oil or melted butter, for drizzling

method

Heat a frying pan, add the oil, brown the butter and sauté the mushrooms, garlic and ginger.

Strain the fat and season the mushrooms with salt, pepper and oregano.

Mix through the cheeses and spring onion and mould the mixture into 80 g balls.

Roll out the pasta on a lightly floured surface into two 5 cm wide x 1 m long strips. Place the first strip on a floured surface, brush lightly with egg or water and place the mushroom balls at 5 cm intervals.

Place the second pasta sheet on top and gently press over the mushroom mixture. Remove all the air around the mushroom ball.

Use a cookie cutter to cut out the ravioli. Cut the pasta 1–2 cm larger than the mushroom ball and squeeze the edges gently to prevent it from opening.

Place in boiling water for a minute or two until cooked. A good indication that they are done is when they float to the surface.

Serve sprinkled with spring onions, freshly grated Parmesan and good olive oil or melted butter.

Pappardelle
with roasted butternut, feta and pumpkin seeds

Pappardelle is pasta cut into 5 cm wide strips.

SERVES: 2–3

PAPPARDELLE
ingredients

½ quantity egg yolk pasta dough 2
(see recipe on page 249)

cake flower or semolina, for dusting

method

Roll out the dough to the last setting on the machine and cut into 15 cm long x 5 cm wide strips. Toss in semolina and blanch in boiling water for 3 minutes.

Cook the pasta just before serving. Prepare the butternut first.

BUTTERNUT
ingredients

1 cup (250 ml) diced butternut

pinch of finely chopped fresh rosemary

½ tsp (2.5 ml) freshly ground black pepper

salt

½ tsp (2.5 ml) lemon zest

1 tsp (5 ml) lemon juice

2 Tbsp (30 ml) butter or olive oil

¼ cup (60 ml) soft sheep's cheese, feta or other cheese of choice, crumbled

3 Tbsp (45 ml) pumpkin seeds, toasted

good-quality olive oil or lemon-infused olive oil, for serving

rocket and large bunch fresh sweet basil, for serving

method

Mix the butternut, rosemary, pepper, salt, lemon zest, lemon juice and butter or olive oil in an ovenproof dish and roast in a wood oven until golden and just tender. Alternatively, wrap these same ingredients in foil and place in warm ash until cooked. (You can also grill it under a medium-hot grill in a conventional oven for about 40 minutes.)

Toss the blanched pasta and roasted butternut mixture with the sheep's cheese or feta, pumpkin seeds and extra olive oil. Season to taste with salt and pepper.

Top with rocket, torn sweet basil and a drizzle of olive oil.

Pappardelle
with *warmoes*

According to the old Dutch cookbook *De Verstandige Kock* (1668), *warmoes* is a variety of stewed or cooked vegetable leaves. Jan van Riebeeck and later C. Louis Leipoldt referred to *warmoes* in their writings, and the latter was of the opinion that beetroot leaves added something special to this stew. During Jan van Riebeeck's time, beetroot was planted for its leaves.

Warmoes consisted mainly of garden vegetables and wild leaves, such as sorrel, and was thickened with white bread added at the end. We follow Leipoldt's recipe, omitting the white bread and serving it with homemade pasta instead.

SERVES: 4–6

ingredients

1 onion, chopped

1 Tbsp (15 ml) butter

2 cups (500 ml) chopped mixed green leaves (beetroot tops, turnip tops, sorrel, chervil, borage, spinach)

½ cup (125 ml) fresh cream

½ cup (125 ml) pine kernels, toasted, or hazelnuts

freshly grated Parmesan cheese

salt and freshly ground black pepper

method

Prepare the pappardelle as described in Pappardelle with Roasted Butternut, Feta and Pumpkin Seeds on page 179.

Sauté the onion in butter in a large pan.

Add the chopped leaves, give the mixture a few quick stirs to heat it through, but do not let it cook.

Add the cream, nuts and Parmesan to taste and remove from the heat. Stir in the blanched pappardelle and season to taste with salt and pepper.

DESSERT

Initially at the Cape, as in Europe, fruit, nuts and cheese were served after a meal, but over time dessert started to include all kinds of sweet puddings. Up until the twentieth century, baked and steamed puddings were often called plum pudding, even though they may not have contained any plums.

According to John Ayto in *The Diners Dictionary* (1993), the Crusaders brought the first prunes from the Middle East to Europe. Many households in Europe had one or more plum trees in the garden and surplus fruit would have been dried for use in cooking. Later, the use of raisins and currants became fashionable, but the cooks never indicated the change in their recipes and therefore many generations inherited the original recipes containing plums.

Doekpoeding (duff or plum pudding) was part of French cuisine. The Afrikaans name was derived from the word *doek*, which referred to the cloth in which the dough was steamed. It was also called Christmas pudding, for this pudding was associated with Christmas and other important celebrations. Later the cloth was exchanged for other containers, but in the middle of the twentieth century when stoves became commonplace, cooks decided it was easier to bake a pudding in the oven rather than steam it, thus this and other steamed puddings went out of fashion. Previous generations still cherish nostalgic memories of the Christmas pudding which was served with brandy sauce and egg custard.

Blancmange is one of the oldest and most popular desserts. Before the Reformation it was served as a fasting dish, but during the fourteenth century it became sought after as a dessert as served by Taillevent, the French king's chef. Blancmange and its variations remained a firm favourite in South Africa up until the twentieth century.

During the seventeenth and eighteenth centuries, before the existence of commercial leavening agents, *broodpoeding* (bread-and-butter pudding) was just as popular as blancmange and it still features regularly in modern cookbooks.

Souskluitjies (cinnamon dumplings) differed, depending on the cook who made them. In the days before commercial raising agents, some cooks used yeast in their dumplings and then cooked them in a little liquid in a pot with a tight-fitting lid. Others used a mixture of butter and flour mixed with boiling water, or choux pastry, and then cooked small spoonfuls in milk or water. Rice dumplings were just as popular as flour dumplings. Melted butter was poured over the cooked dumplings and then cinnamon sugar was sprinkled over.

Other favourites for those with a sweet tooth included steamed fresh or dried fruit which, like pumpkin fritters, was served as an accompaniment to meat or as a dessert, the latter with custard and/or cream.

Kwartiertertjies
(apple quarters)

The triangle-shaped samoosas of today were created by the ancient Persians, who called them *sanbusak*. These dough parcels with their unusual shape and both sweet and savoury fillings became part of Arab cuisine during the seventh century.

The dough, which was kneaded for a long time to work in sufficient air, was made from flour and water, as for pasta. Thereafter a lengthy process was followed whereby the dough was baked in the form of a large pancake. The thin cooked part was pared away each time and hung up over a stick. When everything was cooked, the dough was cut up into strips that were filled and folded into a triangular shape before being deep-fried in fat or oil.

Cooks are always looking for a shortcut to make tasks easier. Apart from a recipe for ravioli, Thomas van der Noot's cookbook (1510) also contains a recipe for a type of *rabiole* with a sweet apple filling. In his recipe the sweet apple samoosa was called *roffioelen* and used ordinary pasta dough as a shortcut to avoid making the *sanbusak* dough. By the start of the twentieth century at the Cape, very few cooks were still preparing the dough following the old Persian *sanbusak* method.

MAKES: 24–30

ingredients

500 g apples, peeled and cut into cubes

1 cinnamon stick

1 star anise

2 whole cloves

2 tsp (10 ml) rose-water

½ cup (125 ml) sugar

½ quantity basic pasta dough 1 (see recipe on page 249)

sunflower oil, for deep-frying

cinnamon sugar, for dusting

method

Place the apples, whole spices, rose-water and sugar in a saucepan and cook over a low heat until thick and caramelised. Remove the cinnamon, star anise and cloves and discard.

Roll out the dough on a lightly floured surface and cut into 6 x 6 cm squares.

Place a spoonful of apple mixture in the centre of each square.

Brush the outer rim of the dough with water and fold over to make a triangle. Press down to make sure both sides are well stuck together, so that the apple will not ooze out during the frying process. Deep-fry in hot oil for 3–5 minutes, turning regularly, until golden.

Dust with cinnamon sugar and serve warm.

Guava pudding

ingredients

8 ripe guavas, peeled and sliced

8 oranges, peeled and segments removed from pith

2 Tbsp (30 ml) brown sugar

1 glass (200 ml) sweet sherry

¼ glass (50 ml) good-quality brandy

method

Layer the guavas, orange segments and sugar in four cocktail glasses.

Pour the sherry and brandy over and place in the refrigerator for a few hours before serving.

Serve with hot or cold custard.

Hanneli Rupert - Rose

Iced Meringue

Meringues were probably brought to the Cape by the French Huguenots, along with the traditional French dessert *ouefs à la neige* (eggs in snow, or floating islands), which dates from 1653 and is still made today. This recipe for iced meringue is a modern version of an old Cape recipe.

SERVES: 10

PRALINE
ingredients

½ cup (125 ml) sugar

1 Tbsp (15 ml) water

¼ cup (60 ml) toasted almonds

¼ cup (60 ml) toasted hazelnuts

method

Place the sugar and water in a saucepan and cook until the sugar turns a light caramel colour – do not stir it while cooking, as the sugar will crystallise.

Scatter the nuts onto non-stick baking paper and pour the caramel over. Leave to cool and harden. Chop the praline finely and reserve in an airtight container.

MERINGUE
ingredients

6 egg whites

1 cup (250 ml) sugar

1½ cups (375 ml) fresh cream

method

Whisk the egg whites until soft peaks start to form, then slowly start adding the sugar while whisking until all the sugar is incorporated. It should be a shiny, firm meringue.

Fold the chopped praline into the meringue.

Whip the cream to stiff peaks, and then fold it into the meringue mixture. Scoop into 10 cups or moulds and freeze for 12 hours.

Serve with a bitter chocolate ice cream.

Snow pudding

Up until the eighteenth century, gelatin was not used at the Cape. Isinglass was available during the nineteenth century, but it was expensive, even in Europe, and seaweed, hartshorn or calf's foot were used to make jelly.

Originally, snow pudding was prepared by cooking lemon zest or leaves with calf's foot for as long as 16 hours. The liquid was then strained through a cloth and cooked until a strong concentrate formed. The sugar was dissolved in this concentrate, lemon juice added and egg whites folded in, before it was poured into a mould to set in a cool place.

SERVES: 4–6

ingredients

1 Tbsp (15 ml) gelatin powder or use sheets

¼ cup (60 ml) cold water

1 cup (250 ml) boiling water

1 cup (250 ml) sugar

¼ cup (60 ml) lemon juice

zest of 1 lemon

2 egg whites

extra 1 Tbsp (15 ml) sugar

method

Sponge the gelatin in the cold water for a few minutes (to sponge means to sprinkle the gelatin powder over cold water and leave it for 1 minute to allow it to absorb all the water), and then dissolve in the boiling water.

Add the sugar, lemon juice and zest and stir until the sugar dissolves.

Strain the liquid through a sieve and leave to cool.

When it starts to set, whisk the mixture until light and fluffy.

Whisk the egg whites until almost stiff and slowly add the extra sugar. Whisk until a stiff meringue forms. Fold the meringue into the gelatin mixture using a metal spoon.

Pour the mixture into a prepared mould or glasses and leave to set in the refrigerator for 2 hours. Decorate as desired and serve with egg custard.

Basic sugar loaf

Berry and wine mould

Berry and wine mould

WINE JELLY
ingredients

3 cups (750 ml) MCC or other sparkling
wine of choice

4 cups (1 litre) water

1 cup (250 ml) sugar

2 cups (2 x 250 ml) strawberries, hulled and halved

1 vanilla pod

¼ cup (60 ml) mint

½ cup (125 ml) gelatin powder per 8 cups
(1.5 litres) of liquid (sponge ½ cup [125 ml]
gelatin in ¾ cup [190 ml] water)

method

Place the sparkling wine, water, sugar, strawberries,
vanilla pod and mint in a bowl, cover with plastic
wrap and place over a pot of simmering water for
45 minutes. Strain through cheesecloth. Add the
sponged gelatin and stir until dissolved.

ingredients

2 cups (2 x 250 ml) raspberries

1 cup (250 ml) blueberries

1 cup (250 ml) gooseberries

wine jelly

method

Line a large terrine dish with plastic wrap. Arrange
half of the berries on the bottom of the mould and
fill halfway with the wine jelly. Refrigerate until set.

Repeat the process with the other half of the
berries and the jelly, and refrigerate until set.

Turn out the jelly mould onto a serving dish and
decorate. Or, for individual portions, slice with a
warm knife and serve with a berry coulis and a slice
of Sugar Loaf (see recipe on page 225).

NOTE:
You can substitute any berries of your
choice, such as mulberries, blackberries or
strawberries.

Rice pudding

Rice and sago pudding are still made today. These dishes were sometimes served with *moskonfyt*, honey or sugarbush syrup, but most of the time, as is the case today, they were served with custard. During the seventeenth century it would have been egg custard, but modern cooks often use shop-bought custard powder to prepare custard or they buy the ready-made product.

SERVES: 4

ingredients

2 cups (500 ml) milk or fresh cream

1 cup (250 ml) cooked rice

1 Tbsp (15 ml) butter

pinch of salt

2 eggs, separated

½ cup (125 ml) sugar

1 piece dried naartjie peel, finely chopped, or zest of 1 fresh lemon, or 2 tsp (10 ml) rose-water

¼ cup (60 ml) mixed berries

method

Preheat the oven to 150 °C (300 °F).

Heat the milk or cream in a saucepan and add the rice. Add the butter and salt.

Whisk the egg yolks with the sugar until light and fluffy. Add the warm milk mixture and beat well.

Beat the egg whites until stiff and fold into the milk mixture. Add the peel, zest or rose-water, and mixed berries.

Pour the mixture into a greased ovenproof dish and bake for 30–40 minutes, or until set.

Serve with *moskonfyt.*

Melon soup

Jan van Riebeeck planted the first melons at the Cape. In the Netherlands and later at the Cape, the fruit was served thinly sliced and eaten with salt and sometimes with pepper.

As an interesting aside, the first melons harvested at the Cape were quite small and, in 1659, Jan van Riebeeck declared that a melon could be sold for a quarter penny if it was ripe and weighed at least a pound (450 g).

This recipe is an example of the sweet soups of the seventeenth century.

SERVES: 6

ingredients

1 sweet melon

7 Tbsp (105 ml) sweet dessert wine or sherry

2 sprigs fresh mint

1 cup (250 ml) fresh cream

1 cup (250 ml) finely diced fresh seasonal fruit

chopped fresh mint, for garnishing

method

Peel the melon and purée the flesh in a blender with the wine until smooth. Add the mint and refrigerate overnight.

The following day, remove the mint and add the cream.

Scoop ¼ cup (60 ml) of the fresh diced fruit into a soup plate.

Pour the melon soup over and garnish with chopped mint.

Fruit consommé

ingredients

6 peaches, peeled and diced, plus 1 for garnishing

⅔ cup (160 ml) fresh orange juice

1 stalk lemon grass, bruised and finely chopped

⅔ cup (160 ml) simple syrup (1 part sugar dissolved in 2 parts water)

¼ cup (60 ml) gooseberries, halved

¼ cup (60 ml) strawberries, diced

¼ cup (60 ml) blackberries, halved

¼ cup (60 ml) blueberries, halved

¼ cup (60 ml) fresh cherries, halved

1 tsp (5 ml) picked fresh thyme leaves

2 Tbsp (30 ml) chopped fresh mint

method

Place the diced peaches, orange juice, lemon grass and syrup in a blender and purée.

Place a layer of cheesecloth in a wire sieve and pour the purée into the sieve. Leave to drain (preferably overnight). Use the strained liquid for the consommé.

The following day, place the fruit and berries in glasses or bowls, pour the consommé over and garnish with mint and diced peach.

NOTE:

Instead of the peaches, use any other fresh, seasonal fruit for the consommé.

Kandeel

Kandeel (caudle) is a delicacy that Jan van Riebeeck refers to in his *Daghregister*. In the Netherlands, it was traditionally served to visitors when a baby was born. This custom was continued at the Cape, where it was served together with biscuits. *Kandeel* probably developed from the Italian *zabayon*, as described in the cookbook *Opera* (1570) by Italian chef Scappi.

A seventeenth-century recipe for *kandeel* lists French wine, water, eggs, cinnamon, cloves and sugar as ingredients. The ingredients were skilfully whisked together into a light and frothy sweet drink. It can also be prepared with more eggs so it can be eaten with a spoon, but it takes an experienced cook to prepare the eggs without the mixture curdling.

SERVES: 2

ingredients

1 cup (250 ml) sweet wine

2 cinnamon sticks

8 whole cloves

pinch of grated nutmeg

1 Tbsp (15 ml) honey

4 egg yolks

method

Place the wine, cinnamon, cloves, nutmeg and honey in a saucepan. Bring to the boil, simmer to infuse and then strain through a fine sieve.

Whisk the egg yolks until light and fluffy and doubled in volume. Whisk in the hot wine mixture, then return all of it to the top of a double boiler (or in a heatproof bowl over simmering water) and continue whisking until it has thickened. Do not leave it unattended in the double boiler, as it will curdle.

Serve while still warm in glasses with little spoons on the side, accompanied by spice biscuits.

If you want to serve it cold, set aside for 15 minutes and then fold in ½ cup (125 ml) whipped cream. Dust with grated nutmeg.

Pancakes

Pancakes are still one of the favourite traditional desserts. At school fêtes, street markets, public gatherings and sports events, the familiar sweet cinnamon smell of freshly cooked pancakes will lure you to the pancake stall, and many people take out the pancake pan at the first sign of the winter chills and rainy weather.

During Jan van Riebeeck's time, sweet and savoury pancakes were popular dishes in the Netherlands. The old recipes instructed that spices such as cloves, nutmeg and mace be included in the dough and only sugar be sprinkled over the baked pancakes. By the twentieth century, the only flavouring used was cinnamon sugar, sprinkled before serving.

Small, paper-thin pancakes were also prepared at the Cape, as in France, but where the French used only a little sauce over their pancakes, at the Cape they were served drenched in sauce. The sauce for the pancakes usually contained sugar, wine, cream and spices, but Van der Hum liqueur, made from brandy, was a favoured ingredient.

SERVES: 4 (8 small pancakes)

PANCAKE BATTER
ingredients

1 cup (250 ml) cake flour

pinch of salt

2 eggs, beaten

2 cups (500 ml) water or milk

2 Tbsp (30 ml) cooking oil or melted butter

method

Sift the flour and salt in a mixing bowl.

Mix into a soft dough with the beaten eggs and small amounts of water or milk at a time. Add the rest of the water and beat briskly.

Add the oil or melted butter and allow to stand for 1 hour.

When ready to cook, drop spoonfuls of batter into a hot greased pan. Cook until bubbles form on the surface, then turn and cook the other side.

Roll up or fold into triangles and serve with slices of lemon and cinnamon sugar, or with Van der Hum Sauce and chocolate curls.

VAN DER HUM SAUCE
ingredients

1 cup (250 ml) water

1 cup (250 ml) sugar

zest of 1 naartjie or orange

2 whole cloves

2 Tbsp (30 ml) butter

½ cup (125 ml) Van der Hum liqueur

1 tsp (5 ml) sherry

2 tsp (10 ml) cream

method

Pour the water into a saucepan over high heat. Add the sugar and stir until it dissolves. Add the zest and cloves and reduce to two-thirds.

Beat in the butter.

Add the Van der Hum liqueur, sherry and cream and pour the hot sauce over the pancakes just before serving.

BAKING

It is impressive how many baked products of excellent quality were prepared at the Cape during the seventeenth and eighteenth centuries when many cooks did not have ovens. Pots and pans with tight-fitting lids were used and coals were placed on top and underneath to provide the heat. You had to be an experienced baker to estimate the correct temperature in order for your creation not to come out as a burnt mess!

This wasn't the only problem when it came to baking in those days. There were no commercial raising agents available and without yeast or must it was crucial to knead or beat sufficient air into the batter for a cake to make it rise. A recipe from 1650 for almond bread instructed that the mixture of flour, sugar and eggs be beaten for 3 hours before adding the almonds.

The first commercial leavening agents – potash and sal volatile – became available towards the end of the eighteenth century and were used mainly for baking biscuits. Using too little of either of these products didn't make the cake rise and too much caused a soapy aftertaste. Royal baking powder was the first successful commercial leavening agent (1873) and was created in America. In this book the old recipes have been adapted to use modern raising agents.

The first commercial flavourings – vanilla and lemon essence – became available towards the end of the nineteenth century. Cooks used lemon and naartjie peel, spices such as ginger, cloves, aniseed, allspice and cinnamon, as well as homemade orange blossom- and rose-water to flavour their desserts. When Jan van Riebeeck planted the fragrant Damask roses (*Rosa gallica* var. *damascena*) at the Cape in 1658, it wasn't for cut flowers or to use the leaves in salads, but rather for making rose-water. Often notices were put up near the Castle in Cape Town, asking women to bring enough rose-water for exporting to Batavia. When enough rose-water could not be supplied, the flowers were shipped in barrels, with salt between the layers, in order for those on the receiving end to prepare the rose-water themselves.

The Dutch syrup cake evolved into *koeksisters* at the Cape and they are still enjoyed today, as are *bolle/bollas*. Other old-time Cape favourites that remain popular are *poffertjies* (puffs) made from choux pastry, pumpkin fritters and pumpkin pie, *tamboesies*, *kolwyntjies* (cup cakes) and Cape brandy tart.

Apple tart

Good-quality tarts didn't need raising agents and, as with the Netherlands, the Cape was famous for its fresh and dried fruit tarts. In the Netherlands, apple tart was the favourite, but at the Cape apricot jam tarts and *melktert* (milk tart) became popular. There was even a *melktert* baked with a topping of apricot halves. *Melktert* with flaky pastry and no topping eventually became part of the traditional cuisine at the Cape. This apple tart is based on a recipe recorded by Thomas van der Noot (1510).

SERVES: 6–8

ingredients

3 large Granny Smith apples, peeled, cored and diced

2 Tbsp (30 ml) sweet wine

½ cup (125 ml) sugar

¼ tsp (1 ml) ground ginger

pinch of ground cloves

1 cinnamon stick

3 cardamom pods, bruised and tied in a muslin cloth

¼ tsp (1 ml) grated nutmeg

2 Tbsp (30 ml) butter

2 Tbsp (30 ml) currants (optional)

½ cup (125 ml) almonds or walnuts, chopped (optional)

3 eggs, separated

½ quantity sweet shortcrust pastry (see recipe on page 252)

cinnamon sugar, for dusting

whipped cream, for serving

method

Preheat the oven to 180 °C (350 °F).

Steam the apples in a saucepan with the wine, sugar and spices until soft. Remove the cinnamon stick and cardamom and discard.

Add the butter, currants and nuts (if using). Leave to cool slightly, before whisking in the egg yolks.

Beat the egg whites until stiff, and then fold in using a metal spoon.

Line a 22 cm pie dish with the sweet shortcrust pastry. Line with parchment (baking) paper, fill with dried beans and bake blind for 15 minutes.

Remove the paper and beans and leave to cool slightly. Pour in the filling and bake for 35–40 minutes.

Dust with cinnamon sugar and serve with whipped cream.

Cheese tart

This recipe doesn't contain sugar, but the cheesecake can be served with preserved maketane, green figs or a liberal drizzling of honey on top. Even berries will be a good accompaniment.

ingredients

butter, for greasing

1 pkt (200 g) digestive biscuits

pinch of ground cinnamon

¼ cup (60 ml) butter

¼ cup (60 ml) cake flour

1 cup (250 ml) milk

1 cup (250 ml) apple juice

1 cup (250 ml) cream cheese

2½ Tbsp (37.5 ml) ricotta cheese

2½ Tbsp (37.5 ml) goat's cheese

2 Tbsp (30 ml) lemon juice

6 eggs, separated

½ tsp (2.5 ml) salt

pinch of white pepper

method

Preheat the oven to 180 °C (350 °F). Grease a 20 cm baking dish with butter.

Crush the digestive biscuits, mix with the cinnamon and use the mixture to dust the greased baking dish.

Melt the butter and add the flour. Gradually add the milk and apple juice and cook over medium heat for 10 minutes.

Add the cream cheese, ricotta and goat's cheese and stir until melted. Add the lemon juice.

Remove from the heat and stir in the egg yolks. Season with salt and pepper.

Whisk the egg whites until stiff, and then fold into the mixture.

Pour the cheese mixture on top of the biscuit crust. Place the dish in an oven pan on top of a dishcloth and pour boiling water into the pan until it reaches halfway up the sides of the dish. Bake for 40 minutes until firm to the touch.

Serve with preserves.

Soetkoekies

Almond and apricot tart

Kaiing (crackling) biscuits

Almond
and apricot tart

In the original recipe the dough was rolled out and baked in two circles, but we find it easier to simply grate it.

MAKES: 1 x 18 cm tart or 24 small tarts

ingredients

200 g butter

2 Tbsp (30 ml) castor sugar

2 Tbsp (30 ml) cooking fat or butter

½ tsp (2.5 ml) vanilla seeds scraped from ⅓ vanilla pod, or rose-water

2 eggs, beaten

2 cups (500 ml) cake flour

½ cup (125 ml) ground almonds

2 tsp (10 ml) baking powder

pinch of salt

½ cup (125 ml) apricot jam

method

Preheat the oven to 180 °C (350 °F).

Cream the butter, sugar, cooking fat or butter and vanilla seeds or rosewater.

Stir in the egg and sift in the flour, ground almonds, baking powder and salt. Knead the dough well.

Grate half of the dough onto the base of a greased 18 cm loose-bottomed cake pan (or two greased cupcake pans for 24 tarts).

Spoon teaspoonfuls of apricot jam over and spread flat. Grate the rest of the dough over.

Bake for 40 minutes (25–30 minutes for small tarts), or until golden brown and set.

NOTE:

About 5 minutes before the end of the baking time, remove the tart(s) from the oven and brush with melted apricot jam. Sprinkle 100 g ground almonds over the top and place back into the oven for 5 minutes until golden brown.

Kaiing
(crackling) biscuits

ingredients

4 cups (4 x 250 ml) cake flour

2 tsp (10 ml) cream of tartar

1 tsp (5 ml) bicarbonate of soda

pinch of salt

½ tsp (2.5 ml) ground cinnamon

½ tsp (2.5 ml) ground ginger

2 cups (500 ml) castor sugar

zest of 1 lemon or naartjie

2 cups (500 ml) *kaiings* (crisply fried sheep's tail fat), minced

3 eggs, whisked

method

Preheat the oven to 180 °C (350 °F).

Sift the cake flour, cream of tartar, bicarbonate of soda, salt, cinnamon and ginger together. Mix in the sugar and lemon or naartjie zest.

Add the *kaiings* and eggs and knead to form a stiff dough. Let it rest for 30 minutes.

Roll the dough into little balls and place on a greased baking tray. Flatten slightly with a fork.

Bake for 10–15 minutes until golden brown.

Photograph on page 214

NOTE:

Crackling here refers to rendered pork or mutton fat that is then minced.

Soetkoekies

The first biscuits made at the Cape during Jan van Riebeeck's time were *krakelinge* in the shape of a number eight, but they have disappeared from modern cooking. Other biscuits such as *soetkoekies* (spice biscuits) and ginger biscuits developed from the small, dry biscuits favoured by the Dutch settlers at the Cape.

MAKES: ± 30 biscuits

ingredients

4 cups (4 x 250 ml) cake flour

½ tsp (2.5 ml) salt

1 tsp (5 ml) ground cinnamon

1 tsp (5 ml) ground cloves

1 tsp (5 ml) ground ginger

1½ cups (375 ml) sugar

1 cup (250 ml) butter

¼ cup (60 ml) cooking fat

1 tsp (5 ml) bicarbonate of soda

2 Tbsp (30 ml) lukewarm water

1 egg, beaten

method

Sift the flour, salt and spices together. Add the sugar.

Rub in the butter and fat until the mixture resembles breadcrumbs.

Dissolve the bicarbonate of soda in the water and add to the beaten egg.

Add the egg mixture to the flour mixture to make a dough. Knead until thoroughly mixed. Leave to stand overnight.

The following day, preheat the oven to 200 °C (400 °F).

Roll out the dough on a lightly floured surface to a thickness of 5 mm. Cut out rounds with a cookie cutter and place on a greased baking tray. Bake for 10 minutes.

Place the biscuits on a wire rack to cool.

Photograph on page 214

Citron tart

The original recipe used cake flour or eggs as thickening agents. We adapted the recipe for today's modern cook and use egg yolks.

SERVES: 8

ingredients

2¼ cups (560 ml) sugar

½ cup (125 ml) water

1 Tbsp (15 ml) butter

½ cup (125 ml) ground almonds

½ cup (125 ml) fine biscuit crumbs

2 eggs plus 2 egg yolks

2 cups (500 ml) citron preserve, chopped

1 ready-made 18 cm shortcrust pie casing or line a pie dish with sweet shortcrust pastry, page 252, and bake blind for 30 minutes at 200 °C (400 °F)

clementine preserve and pouring cream, for serving

method

Preheat the oven to 150 °C (300 °F).

Place the sugar and water in a saucepan over medium heat. Keep stirring until the sugar dissolves. Bring to the boil and reduce to a thick syrup.

Add the butter, almonds and biscuit crumbs. Remove from the heat and let it cool slightly.

Stir in the eggs, egg yolks and citron preserve.

Scoop the filling into the pie casing and bake for 45 minutes, or until firm.

Serve at room temperature with clementine preserve and pouring cream.

Almond cake

ingredients

450 g butter

2 cups (500 ml) sugar

2 cups (500 ml) almonds, chopped

6 eggs, separated

1 tsp (5 ml) bicarbonate of soda

½ cup (125 ml) buttermilk

4 cups (4 x 250 ml) cake flour

pinch of salt

1½ tsp (7.5 ml) cream of tartar

1 Tbsp (15 ml) lemon juice

zest of 1 lemon

method

Preheat the oven to 180 °C (350 °F).

Cream the butter and sugar together. Fold in the almonds.

Add the egg yolks and whisk well.

Mix the bicarbonate of soda with the buttermilk and add it to the egg mixture.

Sift the flour, salt and cream of tartar together and fold into the mixture.

Whisk the egg whites until stiff, and then fold in, along with the lemon juice and zest.

Pour the mixture into a greased and lined 20 cm cake pan and bake for 30–40 minutes.

Let it cool slightly before taking it out of the cake pan.

Serve at room temperature with whipped cream flavoured with rose-water.

Cape brandy tart

Tart
ingredients

1 tsp (5 ml) bicarbonate of soda

1 pkt (250 g) pitted dates, diced

½ cup (125 ml) seedless raisins

1 cup (250 ml) boiling water

½ cup (125 ml) butter

1 cup (250 ml) sugar

1 egg

1¼ cups (300 ml) cake flour

pinch of salt

½ tsp (2.5 ml) baking powder

½ cup (125 ml) pecan nuts, chopped

method

Preheat the oven to 180 °C (350 °F).

Sprinkle the bicarbonate of soda over the dates and raisins and then pour the boiling water over. Set aside.

Cream the butter and sugar in a mixing bowl until light and creamy. Beat in the egg.

Sift the dry ingredients together, and then fold into the butter mixture along with the soaked dates and raisins.

Add the nuts and pour the batter into a greased 25 cm pie dish. Bake for 40–50 minutes until dark brown.

Brandy sauce
ingredients

¾ cup (190 ml) sugar

¾ cup (190 ml) water

1 Tbsp (15 ml) butter

1 tsp (5 ml) vanilla essence or ½ scraped vanilla pod

½ cup (125 ml) brandy

method

Place the sugar, water and butter in a saucepan over high heat and bring to the boil.

Remove from the heat and stir in the vanilla and brandy.

Pour the warm sauce over the tart as soon as it comes out of the oven. Serve hot with whipped cream.

Basic sugar loaf

ingredients

2 large eggs, separated

¼ cup (60 ml) cold orange juice, or rose-water, almond-water or lemon juice

1 tsp (5 ml) orange zest

1 cup (250 ml) castor sugar

1 cup (250 ml) cake flour, sifted 3 times

1 tsp (5 ml) baking powder, sifted 3 times with the flour

pinch of salt

method

Preheat the oven to 180 °C (350 °F).

Beat the egg yolks well. Add the orange juice, rose-water, almond-water or lemon juice and orange zest and beat well again.

Add spoonfuls of castor sugar at a time, continuing to beat the mixture until all the sugar has dissolved and the mixture is light and foamy.

Fold in the flour, baking powder and salt.

Whisk the egg whites until stiff and dry, and then fold into the mixture.

Scoop the batter into a greased loaf pan and bake for 30 minutes, or until done. Remove from the oven, turn out of the pan and cool on a wire rack.

Serve slices with whole fig preserve, *makataan* (wild melon) or grape preserve.

Photograph on page 194

Ginger cake

ingredients

1 cup (250 ml) brown sugar

180 g butter

2 eggs

1 cup (250 ml) golden syrup

3 cups (750 ml) cake flour

1 tsp (5 ml) salt

2 tsp (10 ml) bicarbonate of soda

1 cup (250 ml) sour milk or buttermilk

½ cup (125 ml) preserved ginger, chopped

method

Preheat the oven to 160 °C (325 °F).

Cream the sugar and butter and add the eggs, one at a time, beating well after each addition.

Add the golden syrup and beat well. Sift the flour and salt over; do not mix in yet.

Dissolve the bicarbonate of soda in the milk or buttermilk, pour over the flour mixture and fold in.

Fold in the preserved ginger.

Pour the batter into a greased 20 cm cake pan and bake for about 45 minutes. Check on the cake regularly, as it burns easily.

Remove from the oven and leave to cool in the pan (it is very crumbly while still hot).

Serve topped with butter icing or *makataan* (wild melon) preserve.

Kolwyntjies

The Dutch brought *kollebijne/colombyntjes* (cupcakes) to the Cape during the seventeenth century, where they became known as *kolwyntjies*.

Before electric ovens were commonly used, the cupcakes were baked in a special pan with coals placed on top of the lid and underneath the pan.

MAKES: ± 24

ingredients

½ cup (125 ml) butter

½ cup (125 ml) sugar

1 egg

2 Tbsp (30 ml) milk

1 tsp (5 ml) vanilla essence

2 cups (500 ml) cake flour

1½ tsp (7.5 ml) baking powder

¼ tsp (1 ml) bicarbonate of soda

½ tsp (2.5 ml) salt

¼ tsp (1 ml) grated nutmeg

¾ cup (190 ml) raisins or currants

icing sugar, for dusting

method

Preheat the oven to 180 °C (350 °F).

Whisk the butter and sugar together until light and fluffy.

Whisk the egg with the milk and vanilla essence. Add to the butter mixture.

Sift the dry ingredients together and fold into the butter mixture.

Fold in the raisins or currants.

Scoop large spoonfuls into two greased cupcake pans and bake for 10 minutes. Remove from the oven and place on a wire rack to cool.

Dust with icing sugar and serve.

Makrolle
(Macaroons)

The art of baking macaroons was brought to the Cape by the French Huguenots. It is still part of French cuisine, but although it was one of the favourite small biscuits baked at the Cape from the seventeenth century up to the twentieth century, very few South Africans recognise it as part of traditional food. Recipes for these biscuits appear in various old Cape cookbooks, some with variations containing coconut.

MAKES: 24 double macaroons

MACAROONS
ingredients

2 cups (500 ml) ground almonds

1¼ cups (300 ml) castor sugar

4 egg whites

pinch of salt

1 tsp (5 ml) rose-water

method

Dry the almonds overnight in a 70 °C (160 °F) oven.

The following day, increase the oven temperature to 150 °C (300 °F).

Put the almonds and sugar in a saucepan over medium heat until the sugar has melted. Do not stir, as the sugar will crystallise.

Take the almond-sugar mixture off the stove and let it cool slightly.

Whisk the egg whites with the salt until soft peaks form. Fold this into the almond and sugar mixture, and then fold in the rose-water.

Layer a baking tray with greaseproof paper and butter the paper.

Spoon the biscuit mixture into a piping bag and pipe small rounds (about the size of a teaspoon) onto the buttered paper, about 3 cm apart.

Bake for 20–30 minutes. Remove from the oven and lift from the baking tray while still hot. Place on a wire rack to cool.

GANACHE
ingredients

7 Tbsp (105 ml) fresh cream

¼ cup (60 ml) white chocolate

method

Bring the cream just to boiling point.

Chop the chocolate finely and place in a heatproof bowl.

Pour the boiling cream over and stir until the chocolate has melted. Leave to cool slightly.

Sandwich the macaroons together with 1 tsp (5 ml) ganache.

Oblietjies

The Dutch brought *oblietjies* to the Cape. Initially these small waffles were baked in a small iron pan with a lid, called an *oblie-yster* (oblie iron). The pan usually had an engraved pattern, which decorated the *oblietjies* and made them look like little works of art. Because the oblie iron was used on an open fire, it had a very long handle, which made it heavy and difficult to manipulate. When stoves with ovens became commonplace at the Cape, *oblietjies* were baked on a baking tray in the oven and oblie irons and *oblietjies* along with them went out of fashion.

Today, many South Africans do not realise that the erstwhile *oblietjies* and brandy snaps are the same thing.

MAKES: 24 large

ingredients

2 eggs

2¼ cups (560 ml) brown sugar

2 tsp (10 ml) pounded naartjie peel

1 glass (120 ml) sweet wine

2 tsp (10 ml) ground cinnamon

2 cups (500 ml) cake flour

1 cup (250 ml) butter, melted

method

Preheat the oven to 180 °C (350 °F).

Beat the eggs and sugar together. Allow to rest for 10 minutes.

Add the peel, wine and cinnamon.

Sift the flour and fold in alternately with the melted butter.

Roll the dough into little balls (about the size of a teaspoon) and arrange on a greased baking tray, about 3 cm apart. Bake for 10–12 minutes.

As soon as they come out of the oven, roll up immediately into little horn shapes or use the handle of a wooden spoon to make cigar shapes. It is best to do only two at a time, as you have to work quickly. If they become too hard and cold to roll, you can put them back into the oven for a few minutes.

If using an oblie iron, place the dough ball in the centre of the hot iron, press lightly and hold until crisp.

Serve filled with whipped cream and preserved ginger or fresh figs.

Raisin biscuits

MAKES: ±24 large biscuits

ingredients

¾ cup (190 ml) sugar

¾ cup (190 ml) butter or cooking fat,
at room temperature

1 egg

⅔ cup (160 ml) milk

1¾ cup (440 ml) cake flour

1 Tbsp (15 ml) baking powder

pinch of salt

1 cup (250 ml) seedless raisins

½ tsp (2.5 ml) grated nutmeg

method

Preheat the oven to 180 °C (350 °F).

Beat the sugar and butter or cooking fat together. Add the egg and beat well.
Add the milk.

Sift the flour, baking powder and salt together, and then fold it into the
milk mixture.

Add the raisins and nutmeg and fold in.

Bake spoonfuls of the mixture in a greased muffin pan or on a baking tray
for 15–20 minutes.

Remove from the oven and lift from the baking tray while still hot. Place on
a wire rack to cool.

Plum

and frangipane tart

ingredients

¼ quantity flaky pastry (see recipe
on page 253)

method

Preheat the oven to 200 °C (400 °F).

Roll out the pastry on a floured surface to about
4 mm thick. Cut out 10 cm diameter rounds,
place onto a buttered baking tray and bake until
golden brown.

Place another baking tray on top of the rounds
after they are removed from the oven and press
down to flatten the pastry. Place a weight on top
and return to the oven for a further 4 minutes.
Leave to cool.

GLAZE
ingredients

2 Tbsp (30 ml) brandy

2 Tbsp (30 ml) honey

2 Tbsp (30 ml) sugar

2 Tbsp (30 ml) orange juice

method

Place all the ingredients in a saucepan and cook
until it has a syrupy consistency. Keep warm.

FRANGIPANE
ingredients

2 cups (500 ml) butter

2 cups (500 ml) sugar

8 eggs, whisked

2 Tbsp (30 ml) cake flour, sifted

2½ cups (625 ml) ground almonds

method

Beat the butter and sugar together until light and
airy. Add the eggs, one by one, while mixing slowly.
Add the flour and almonds and refrigerate for
2 hours before using.

TO ASSEMBLE
ingredients

12–15 ripe plums, pitted, halved
and sliced 1 mm thick

icing sugar, for dusting

method

Preheat the oven to 220 °C (425 °F).

Spread the frangipane on the pastry discs – about
3 mm thick. Arrange overlapping slices of plums on
the frangipane, all the way around until the pastry is
evenly covered.

Dust with icing sugar and place in the oven for
8–12 minutes or until the frangipane puffs up and
is light brown in colour.

Lightly brush the top with the glaze and serve with
your favourite ice cream (honey ice cream works well).

Pierneef and his daughter
Maria, c1929

BASIC RECIPES

Salted preserved lemons

Slice thinly and add to a summer salad or use in a stir-fry with avocado, greens and fish. Or serve with roasted aubergine and lamb chops or traditional Cape chicken pie.

MAKES: 3 kg

ingredients

3 kg lemons, cut into wedges or quarters

2 cups (500 ml) coarse sea salt

2 cups (500 ml) lemon juice

2 cups (500 ml) water

method

Sterilise 4–6 large glass jars.

Coat the lemon wedges with the salt, and then pack them into the jars and press down. Place a weight on top and leave for 1 week.

Mix the lemon juice and water and pour into the jars.

Leave for at least 1 month before using.

As soon as the lemons are tender and ripe, you can strain off the liquid and place them in newly sterilised jars. Cover with herbs and vegetable oil.

Usually only the lemon peel is used, while the flesh is discarded. However, you can use the flesh to add flavour to soups and fish stock.

Stock

Vegetable nage (stock)

MAKES: 12 cups (3 litres)

ingredients

2 carrots, chopped

2 onions, chopped

1 stalk celery, chopped

1 fennel bulb (including top), chopped

3 cloves garlic, sliced

2 bay leaves

1 tsp (5 ml) fennel seeds

1 tsp (5 ml) coriander seeds

1 tsp (5 ml) cardamom pods

1 tsp (5 ml) cumin seeds

3 star anise

12 cups (3 litres) water

method

Place all the ingredients in a large stockpot or saucepan and bring to the boil. Reduce the heat and simmer for 1 hour.

Remove the pot from the heat and allow to cool, then refrigerate overnight.

The following day, strain the stock through a fine sieve.

This stock freezes well for up to 3 months.

Spiced vegetable

MAKES: 6 cups (1.5 litres)

ingredients

1 bunch fresh thyme, picked

1 bunch fresh marjoram, picked

1 large bunch young beetroot leaves

1 large bunch sorrel

2 medium heads lettuce

100 g green beans

1 bunch spring onions, sliced

100 g sliced green marrow

2 turnips, diced

1 medium fresh green chilli, chopped

1 piece green ginger (available from Asian supermarkets or specialty food stores), or fresh root ginger

mace or nutmeg

peppercorns

method

Place all the ingredients in a stockpot or large saucepan and cover with water.

Bring to the boil, reduce the heat and simmer for 2 hours. Replenish the water as it evaporates.

Strain through a fine sieve.

This stock may be frozen for up to 6 weeks.

Chicken

MAKES: 24 cups (6 litres)

ingredients

1 whole chicken or
2 kg chicken bones

28 cups (7 litres) water

2 stalks celery, chopped

¼ cup (60 ml) celery leaves,
chopped

5 cloves garlic, sliced

1 large leek, sliced

2 onions, chopped

1 Tbsp (15 ml) coriander
seeds

½ cup (125 ml) fresh picked
thyme

method

Place the chicken and water in a large stockpot and bring
to the boil.

Skim the surface until all the sediment is removed, 5–10 minutes.

Add the remaining ingredients and simmer for 2½ hours.

Remove from the heat and leave to cool for 1 hour.

Strain through a fine sieve.

This stock may be frozen for up to 4 weeks.

NOTE:

For a brown chicken stock, chop 4 kg chicken wings
or carcasses and follow the Veal Stock recipe (see
below) — add plenty of thyme and soup celery.

Veal or Beef

MAKES: 32–36 cups (8–9 litres)

ingredients

oil and butter for frying

4 kg meaty veal or beef bones

2 cups (500 ml) diced carrots

2 cups (500 ml) diced onions

1 whole garlic bulb, halved

2 cups (500 ml) good-quality
red wine

40 cups (10 litres) water

5 sprigs fresh rosemary

1 cup (250 ml) dried mushrooms

method

Heat a large heavy-based stockpot or saucepan and
add oil and butter.

Make sure the butter has browned well and then add
the bones and fry until dark brown.

Add the carrots, onions and garlic and cook until the onions
are golden brown.

Pour the contents of the pot through a strainer or
colander to remove all the fat.

Place the meat and vegetables back in the pot, add the red wine
and cook to a syrup.

Add the water, rosemary and mushrooms and simmer for 6–8 hours
or 4 hours in a pressure cooker. Skim the surface regularly.

Strain the stock through a fine sieve and pour back into the pot.
Bring to the boil and simmer for 15 minutes, skimming the surface.

Strain the stock for a final time through muslin cloth (or an
old pillowcase).

This stock may be frozen for up to 4 weeks.

Lamb

Follow the same recipe as for Veal Stock, but use lamb
knuckle and rib bones instead of veal bones.

243

Venison

ingredients

5 Tbsp (75 ml) vegetable oil

3 Tbsp (45 ml) butter

reserved neck bones, chopped into 2 cm pieces

2 carrots, chopped

1 onion, chopped

2 cloves garlic

1 cup (250 ml) good-quality red wine

16 cups (4 litres) water

2 sprigs fresh oregano or marjoram

1 Tbsp (15 ml) juniper berries

2 bay leaves

½ cup (125 ml) dried mushrooms

method

Heat a large frying pan and heat the oil to almost smoking point.

Add the butter and bones. Fry for 15 minutes while stirring, until the bones are dark brown.

Add the carrots, onion and garlic and cook for a further 10 minutes until all the vegetables are lightly caramelised.

Strain off all the fat and place the bones and vegetables in a large stockpot or saucepan.

Add the red wine, water, herbs, berries, bay leaves and mushrooms and bring to the boil.

Reduce the heat and simmer for 3 hours, skimming the surface every 10 minutes.

Strain the stock through a fine sieve and freeze for up to 4 weeks.

Fish

ingredients

2 Tbsp (30 ml) olive oil

3 onions, sliced

3 leeks, sliced

1 fennel bulb, sliced

3 stalks celery, sliced

3 bay leaves

½ cup (125 ml) fresh parsley

½ cup (125 ml) fresh basil leaves

1 sprig fresh tarragon, or 1 tsp (5 ml) dried

1 Tbsp (15 ml) coriander seeds

1 tsp (5 ml) white peppercorns

3 kg fish bones, rinsed well (preferably flat fish such as sole)

2 cups (500 ml) dry white wine

10 tsp (50 ml) pastis (Ricard or Pernod)

28 cups (7 litres) water

method

Heat the olive oil in a large stockpot or saucepan and add all the vegetables, herbs, coriander and peppercorns. Sauté until tender.

Add the fish bones and cook for 5 minutes.

Add the remaining ingredients and simmer for 2 hours.

Strain through a muslin cloth.

Shellfish *nage* (stock)

ingredients

3 Tbsp (45 ml) olive oil

1 carrot, chopped

2 tomatoes, chopped

2 stalks celery, chopped

1 fennel bulb, chopped

1 onion, chopped

4-cm piece fresh root ginger, peeled and chopped

3 cloves garlic, chopped

1 stalk lemon grass, chopped

½ cup (125 ml) fresh basil leaves

½ cup (125 ml) fresh coriander leaves

pinch of saffron

2 bay leaves

4 cups (4 x 250 ml) reserved shells from prawns and crayfish

1 cup (250 ml) dry white wine

8 cups (2 litres) water

method

Heat a stockpot or large saucepan and add the olive oil.

Add all the ingredients, except the shells, wine and water, and sauté for 5 minutes until softened.

Place the shells in a blender or food processor and blend to a paste.

Add the shell paste to the pot and sauté for 2 minutes.

Add the wine and water and simmer very slowly for 1 hour. Do not let it boil.

Remove from the heat and leave to stand for 1 hour to allow the sediment to settle.

Strain the stock from the top, spooning it out with a ladle, and pass through a muslin cloth.

This stock may be frozen for up to 4 weeks.

Mushroom

ingredients

1 cup (250 ml) dried mushrooms

2 Tbsp (30 ml) olive oil

1 cup (250 ml) forest or brown mushrooms, chopped

1 onion, chopped

1 stalk celery, sliced

4 cloves garlic, sliced

5 sprigs fresh thyme

8 cups (2 litres) vegetable stock (see recipe on page 242) or water

method

Preheat the oven to 180 °C (350 °F).

Place the dried mushrooms on a baking tray and roast for about 4 minutes until fragrant.

Heat a large saucepan and add the olive oil.

Fry the fresh mushrooms until golden brown. Reduce the heat and add the onion, celery, garlic and thyme. Sweat until soft.

Add the stock or water and dried roasted mushrooms and simmer for 30 minutes, replenishing any stock that evaporates.

Remove from the heat, leave to cool, and then store in the refrigerator overnight to infuse.

Strain through a fine sieve.

This stock freezes well for up to 6 months.

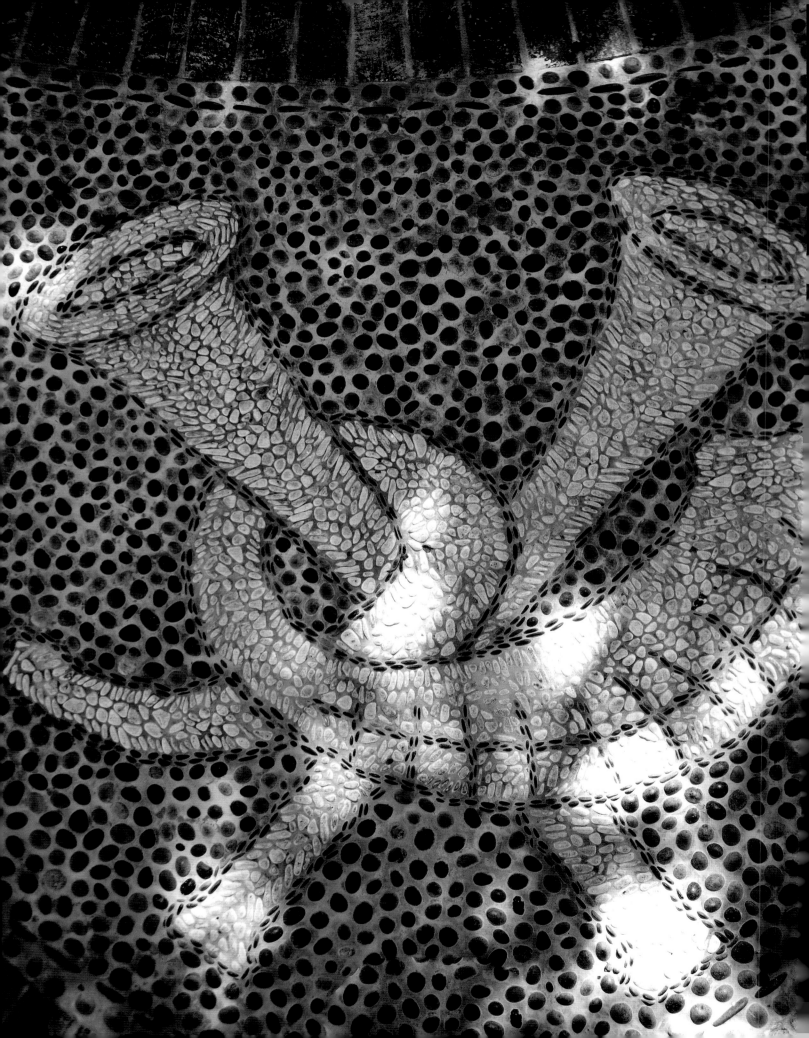

Soup flavouring

This is an old-fashioned recipe that we rediscovered and it is quite useful to keep on hand. Use 2 Tbsp (30 ml) per 2 cups (500 ml) soup.

MAKES: just over 2 cups (550 ml)

ingredients

½ cup (125 ml) brown sugar

1 Tbsp (15 ml) water

2 cups (500 ml) good-quality red wine

1 tsp (5 ml) lemon zest

6 wholes cloves

1 blade of mace or ½ tsp (2.5 ml) grated nutmeg

1 onion, chopped

2 Tbsp (30 ml) tomato sauce or paste

method

Place the sugar and water in a saucepan and heat until the sugar has dissolved.

Add the remaining ingredients, bring to the boil and cook until the onion is tender.

Strain and bottle.

It will keep for up to 2 weeks in the refrigerator.

Curry mixes

Curry mix 1 (for fish)

MAKES: ± 300 ml

ingredients

170 g turmeric

280 g coriander seeds

7 g cumin

140 g ground ginger

28 g cayenne pepper

1 bay leaf

1 cloves

method

Mix all the ingredients together.

Store in an airtight container.

Curry mix 2 (fragrant)

MAKES: ½ cup (125 ml)

ingredients

45 g coriander seeds

45 g cumin seeds

45 g ground ginger

15 g freshly ground black pepper

90 g turmeric

15 g cayenne pepper

pinch of saffron

1 cardamom pod

1 small cinnamon stick

herbs and aromatics of your choice

method

Mix all the ingredients together.

Store in an airtight container.

Curry mix 3 (for meat)

MAKES: just over ½ cup (150 ml)

ingredients

90 g coriander seeds

90 g turmeric

30 g freshly ground black pepper

15 g cayenne pepper

15 g mustard powder

15 g ground ginger

15 g ground cardamom

15 g ground cinnamon

15 g cumin seeds

method

Mix all the ingredients together.

Store in an airtight container.

NOTE:

Rather make your curry mix fresh every time for a better quality curry.

Toast your curry mix in a pan until fragrant before using.

Pasta dough

BASIC

MAKES: 800 g (4 portions)

ingredients

1 small pkt (500 g) '00' pasta flour or finest quality cake flour

5 eggs

1 Tbsp (15 ml) olive oil

½ tsp (2.5 ml) salt

1 tsp (5 ml) iced water

method

Mix all the ingredients together to make a firm dough and knead for 5 minutes.

Refrigerate for 1 hour before use.

WITH EGG YOLKS

MAKES: 900 g (4 large portions)

ingredients

1 small pkt (500 g) '00' pasta flour or finest quality cake flour

12 egg yolks

2 eggs

pinch of saffron

2 Tbsp (30 ml) olive oil

1 tsp (5 ml) salt

method

Mix all the ingredients together to make a firm dough and knead well.

Refrigerate for 1 hour before use.

NOTE:

Keep pasta dough wrapped in plastic wrap to prevent drying out and discoloration.

The pasta dough can be frozen for up to 1 month.

You can dry and powder tomato skins for a tomato-flavoured dough — add 1 Tbsp (15 ml) per 250 g flour. (You can also use dried pulverised mushrooms.)

Pastry

Sweet shortcrust

MAKES: 1.1 kg or 3½ cups

ingredients

300 g butter

150 g sugar

2 eggs

2 egg yolks

1 small pkt (500 g) cake flour

pinch of salt

method

Cream the butter and the sugar until light and fluffy.

Add the eggs and yolks one by one until incorporated.

Sift in the flour and salt and mix to form a dough. Form into a ball and wrap in plastic wrap.

Rest for 1 hour in the refrigerator before using.

Savoury shortcrust

MAKES: 1.4 kg or 4½ cups

ingredients

3¼ cups (810 ml) cake flour

1 tsp (5 ml) salt

2½ tsp (12.5 ml) baking powder

¼ tsp (1 ml) cream of tartar

¼ cup (60 ml) butter

¾ cup (190 ml) suet fat or Holsum baking fat

1 cup (250 ml) iced water

1 egg

2 Tbsp (30 ml) white wine vinegar

method

Sift the cake flour, salt, baking powder and cream of tartar.

Rub in the butter and fat to form a crumbly texture.

Mix the water, egg and vinegar together and mix into the dry ingredients to form a dough.

Form into a ball and wrap in plastic wrap.

Rest for 20 minutes in the refrigerator before using.

Flaky pastry

ingredients

2 cups (500 ml) cake flour

1 tsp (5 ml) salt

250 g cold butter

just over ½ cup (150 ml) cold water

method

Sift the flour and salt together in a mixing bowl.

Roughly break the butter into the flour and rub it in a little. There should still be bits of butter visible.

Add two-thirds of the water and form a rough dough. Add more water if needed.

Wrap the dough in plastic wrap and rest in the refrigerator for 1 hour.

Roll out the dough on a lightly floured surface, in one direction only and until it forms a rectangle about three times long as it is wide. Try and keep the edges of the pastry as straight as possible. The dough should still have long butter streaks visible.

Fold the top third of the pastry downwards and the bottom third over that. Turn the pastry 90° and roll out to three times its length. Repeat the rolling process twice more, allowing the dough to rest in the refrigerator for 1 hour each time. Rest for 1 hour before using.

Buttermilk pastry

This recipe is an easy alternative to puff or flaky pastry.

ingredients

3 cups (750 ml) cake flour

1 Tbsp (15 ml) sugar

1 tsp (5 ml) salt

1½ Tbsp (22.5 ml) baking powder

1 tsp (5 ml) freshly ground black pepper

1 tsp (5 ml) fresh thyme leaves

¾ cup (190 ml) butter

¾ cup (190 ml) buttermilk

¼ cup (60 ml) milk

1 egg

1 egg yolk

method

Mix all the dry ingredients in a bowl.

Work the butter into the dry mixture using your fingertips until it resembles breadcrumbs.

Mix the buttermilk, milk, egg and yolk together, and then add it to the dry mixture.

Work lightly until it forms a dough – don't overwork it.

Wrap in plastic wrap and rest in the refrigerator for 1 hour before using.

BIBLIOGRAPHY

1. National Archives of South Africa (NASA)

A462, Mrs. M Stewart; A602.9 Hudson; A2415 JW Bell.

2. National Library of South Africa, Cape Town

MSB 837 1 (1); MSB 837 1 (2); MSB 837 1 (3); MSB 837.2 (2); MSB 837.3 (1); MSB 837.3 (3); MSB 837 2 (4); MSB 777 1 (1); MSB 777 1 (3); MSB 777 1 (4); MSB 563 (1); MSB 897; MSB 324; MSC 56 (1); MSC 56 (3).

3. Books available online/internet/websites

- ✍ www.boerboksa.co.za
- ✍ www.coquinaria.nl
- ✍ www.davidfriedman.com
- ✍ www.homemade-dessert-recipes.com
- ✍ www.kookhistorie.nl
- ✍ www.landbou.com
- ✍ www.medievalcookery.com

4. Periodicals

Maandblad: Die Boerevrouw
April, June, July 1919;
May, June, November, December 1920.

5. Books

ALEXANDER COOK, M.
Die Kaapse Kombuis
(Stellenbosch).

ANONYMOUS, (A LADY)
Life at the Cape a hundred years ago (1861)
(Struik, Cape Town, 1963).

APICIUS
- ✍ *The Roman cookery book.*
   Parallel English translation from the ninth century. Latin by Barbara Flower and Elisabeth Rosenbaum (London, 1958).

- ✍ *A critical edition*
   English translation by Christopher Grocock and Sally Grainger
   (Prospect Books, Totnes, Devon, 2006);

BALKEMA, A.A.
The letters of Lady Anne Barnard to Henry Dundas
(Cape Town, 1973).

BARNARD, E.
Outydse reseppies
(Maskew Miller, 1952).

BAUMAN, J. and DE NUYN, P.
Vrolijke Uuren
(Boekverkoper in die Kalverstraat Anno 1681).

BRINK, ANDRÉ P.
Brandewyn in Suid-Afrika
(Cape Town, 1973).

BOSMAN, D.B.
Briewe van Johanna Maria van Riebeeck en ander Riebeeckiana
(Amsterdam, 1952).

BOTHA, C.G.
Social life in the Cape Colony in the 18th Century
(Cape Town, 1926).

BOLSMAN, E.
French footprints in South Africa
(Be My Guest Publishers, Pretoria, 2008).

BUREMA, L.
De voeding in Nederland van de Middeleeuwen tot de twintigste eeuw.

CLAASSENS, H.W.
Die Geskiedenis van Boerekos 1652–1806
(Pretoria, 2006).

COETZEE, R.
The South African Culinary Tradition
(Cape Town, 1981).

CONRADIE, E.
Hollandse skrywers uit Suid-Afrika 1
(Pretoria, 1934).

DEPARTEMENT VAN LANDBOU
Kos en kookkuns
(Pretoria, 1947).

DE JONG, C.
Die lewe van Jan van Riebeeck, 'n skets
(Pretoria, 1980).

DE VILLIERS, A. (Dr)
Volksgebruike uit vervloë dae
(SABC, Johannesburg, 1965).

DE VILLIERS, J.
Namakwaland verhale-resepteboek
(Bellville, 1995).

DE VILLIERS, S.J.A.
Kook en geniet
(Bloemfontein, 1970).

DALBY, A. and GRANGER, S.
The classical cookbook
(London, 2000).

DIJKMAN, E.J.
Die Suid Afrikaanse kook-, koek- en resepteboek
(Human en Rousseau, Cape Town, 1979).

DUCKITT, H.J.
 ✍ *Where is it of recipes* (London, 1891).
 ✍ *Diary of a Cape housekeeper* (London, 1902).

FAULL, L. and VIDA, H.,
Cookery in Southern Africa
(Cape Town, 1970).

FRANKEN, J.L.M.
Duminy-dagboeke
(Van Riebeeck Society, Cape Town, 1938).

FOUCHÉ, L.
Het dagboek van Adam Tas
The Diary of Adam Tas 1705–1706
(London, 1914).

FYNPROEWERSGILDE STELLENBOSCH
So eet ons in Stellenbosch
(Cape Town, 1979).

GERBER, H.
 ✍ *Traditional cookery of the Cape Malays*
     (Cape Town, 1854).

 ✍ *Cape cookery old and new*
     (Howard B. Timmins, Cape Town, 1950).

GRANT, M.
Roman cookery (London, 2008).

GRAINGER, S.
Cooking Apicius (Totnes, Devon, 2006).

GREEN, L.G.
 ✍ *Karoo land van weerbegin*
     (John Malherbe, Cape Town, 1964).
 ✍ *Tavern of the seas*
     (Cape Town, 1975).

HATTERSLEY, A.F.
An Illustrated social history of South Africa
(Cape Town, 1973).

HEWITT, A.G.
Cape cookery
(Cape Town, 1890).

HENRY, R.
Ouma's Cookery book
(Bloemfontein, 1955).

HOFMEYER, D.
'n Boervrou kook met wyn
(Cape Town).

KARSTEN, M.C.
The Old Company's Garden at the Cape
(Maskew Miller, Cape Town, 1951).

KOLBE, P.
Naauwkeurige beschrywing van de Kaap
de Goede Hoop
(I-II Amsterdam, 1727).

KUTTEL, M.
Hildagonda Duckit's book of recipes
(Cape Town, 1966).

LEIPOLDT, C.L.
 ✍ *Kos vir die kenner*
     (Tafelberg, Cape Town, 1978).
 ✍ *Leipoldt's food and wine*
     (Stonewall Books, Cape Town, 2003).
 ✍ *Polfyntjies vir die proe*
     (Cederberg Publishers, 2005).

LICHTENSTEIN, H.
Travels in Southern Africa
(Van Riebeeck Society, Cape Town, 1928).

MEES, W.C.
Maria Queuellerius
(Assen MCMLII).

MENTZEL, O.F.
*A geographical and topographical description
of the Cape of Good Hope,* translation by
H.J. Mandelbrote, G.V. Marais and H. Hoge
(Van Riebeeck Society, Cape Town, 1921, 1925
and 1944).

MUHAMMED B.AL-HUSAN B.MUHAMMAD
B.AL KARÎM
A Baghdad cookery book
(Prospect Books, Devon, 2005)
translation by Charles Perry

OLNEY, R. and GANTIE, J.
Provence the beautiful cookbook
(Leo Books, Cape Town, 1996).

PIENAAR, T.
Kaapse Kontreikos
(Ram Boeke, Cape Town).

ROBINSON, A.M.L.
The letters of Lady Anne Barnard to Henry Dundas
(A.A. Balkema, Cape Town, 1973).

RODINSON MAXIME, ARBERRY A.J.
and PERRY CHARLES
Medieval Arab cookery
(Prospect Books, 2001)

ROOD, B.
 ᔡ *101 Traditional South African Recipes*
  (Tafelberg Publishers, Cape Town, 1977).
 ᔡ *Kos uit die veldkombuis*
  (Kaapstad, 1994).

ROSE, P.G.
The sensible cook
(USA, 1989).

SCAPPI, B.
The Opera of Bartolomeo Scappi (1570),
translation by Terence Scully (Toronto, 2008).

SCHOTEL, G.D.J.
*Het Oud-Hollandse huisgzin
der zeventiende eeuw*
(Haarlem, 1868).

SHAIDA, M.
The legendary cuisine of Persia
(London, 2009).

SLADE, H.M.
Mrs. Slade's South African cookery book
(Central News Agency, 1948).

THE SHELL COMPANY
 ᔡ *Mev Pitte se kookboek* (1937).
 ᔡ *Voortrekker resepte* (1940).

TULLEKEN, S. van H.
Die praktiese kookboek vir Suid-Afrika
(Tafelberg, Cape Town, 1975).

VALENTYN, F.
Beschryvinge van de Kaap der Goede Hoope
(I-II Van Riebeeck Society, second series no. 2
and 4, 1971 and 1973).

VAN NIEKERK, A.A.J.
Herneuter
(Tafelberg, 1975)

VAN ZYL, D.
Afval en afvalligheidjies (1983).

VELDSMAN, P.
Kos van die eeu
(Kaapstad, 1998).

WILLAN, A.
Great cooks and their recipes
(London, 2000).

6. *Unpublished manuscripts*

EKSTEEN, A., *Onthou jy nog.*

VAN SCHALKWYK, E., *Disse uit die Korbeelhuis.*

HERMAN., *Ouma Se Warm Kombuis.*

RECIPE INDEX

T